# How to win at housework

### DON ASLETT

EXLEY

First published in Great Britain
in 1983 by Exley Publications Ltd,
16 Chalk Hill, Watford,
Herts WD1 4BN, United Kingdom.

Reprinted November 1983
Second reprint June 1988

**British Library Cataloguing in
Publication Data**

Don Aslett.
  How to win at housework.
  1. Housework.
  I. Title.
  648    TX324

**ISBN 0-905521-81-1 (Hbk)**
**ISBN 1-85015-011-7 (Pbk)**

First published in the USA
by Writer's Digest Books.

Reproduced, printed and bound in Great Britain by
Hazell Watson & Viney Limited
Member of BPCC plc
Aylesbury, Bucks, England

ILLUSTRATIONS BY DAVID LOCK

# Contents

# Has anyone ever asked you a question about cleaning you couldn't answer?

I can *answer* any cleaning question; however, after twenty-five years of cleaning homes and businesses I realize there are situations that have no simple, neat, revolutionary answer. There are some which have me stumped, to which the answer is just what you thought – i.e., it's a hard tedious job, and there's no magic tip, no 'eureka' solution: 'How do you clean feather pillows? . . . What is a *fast* way to clean ovens? . . . How can I get my children to clean up their rooms? . . . How do you fold fitted sheets neatly?' These are problems to which there is no easy, comforting answer – but there *is* an answer, I assure you. Climatic conditions, standards of personal cleanliness – from picky to piggy – and individual resources vary greatly, but there really are no cleaning problems that can't be answered. Even if that answer has to be 'Get a professional to do it,' or 'Destroy it and buy a new one.' Lack of knowledge about how you can solve a cleaning challenge is not the big problem: lack of determination, nerve, or money to get going is usually what leaves a cleaning mystery unsolved.

The questions in this book don't go into home dishwashing or laundry problems and techniques because I think in those areas most of you could teach me something. And there *are* some things I've never heard of; there is always something new, something unique to an area, that I'm learning about. Once, when I appeared on a local radio phone-in, a lady asked me how to clean vinyl windows, saying hers were foggy. I'd never heard of vinyl windows and thought she might be talking about a type of window called Plexiglas, but she wasn't: it turned out that in warm areas, people use a transparent material they call 'vinyl' to enclose porches and patios. Now I know. (And it can't be cleaned!)

The questions I really *can't* answer, I simply don't dare . . . like 'What can I do about my white velvet chair?' (Good grief, woman – what on earth made you buy such a thing – it's bad enough tackling an earth-brown one . . .) Or, 'How can I get rid of my husband's junk?' (Junk, worthless as it may be, is sacred: don't meddle in it or try to reform it if you're not the owner and originator of the junk. You're asking for trouble.) 'What can I do about the carpets my little dog Marmaduke has messed on?' (I wouldn't touch that one with a ten-foot toilet plunger.) So I come clean and tell them I don't know (but I really do, as you'll find by reading on).

In the years I spent working my way through university I cleaned thousands of homes professionally. And for the last fifteen years I've handled cleaning problems in thousands more homes, plus millions of square feet of commercial buildings. I've brought up six children (and had six teenagers at once) and faced all the real-life challenges a home cleaner does. And I now head one of the largest cleaning firms in the world. Some people

call me the best, an *expert* on cleaning. Well, I do know a lot and have done a lot, but there are hundreds of you who know how to do certain things better and faster than I do. Though I've tried to answer even the toughest questions as fully as possible, my answers aren't the end of the line – the final word – there will be a better answer one day. But please, though I'm not the be-all and end-all of household wisdom, try to read these answers with an open mind (all the way to the end) and you may well learn something truly helpful (if only what *not* to do). Be aware, too, that techniques and approaches to specific cleaning problems can often be applied to very different cleaning situations, so be alert as well as open to new ideas.

Between my successes and my failures, my discoveries and my mistakes (and

what I've *learned* from my mistakes), I can help you cut your cleaning work up to 75 per cent. In my first book, *Is There Life After Housework?*, I tried to express my basic cleaning principles and philosophy. I refer to *Is There Life After Housework?* in this book, whenever I think you might be interested, in more detail, in certain things that I don't want to take the space to repeat here.

I've gathered the questions in this book from all the homemakers I've met on my travels, in my professional work and my personal life. At the housecleaning talks I give, I've asked audiences to pick their most urgent queries. Every day new questions come. In choosing the hundred to include in this book, we've selected not only the ones we thought the average homemaker most needs the answer to, but also questions it's practically impossible to find an answer to anywhere else. We've included a few questions that we wouldn't have otherwise, simply because they're asked so often. And we have even thrown in a few rhetorical questions to help boost your morale in the never-ending war on dirt. (If you have a burning question not included in these pages, please do send it to me so I can be sure to consider it for the *next* edition.)

So THANK YOU for the questions; I hope you enjoy the answers. They should not only bail you out of some tricky cleaning situations, but help you improve the warmth and quality of your life as well.

# Should I dust or vacuum first?

First, if you mat all entrances, inside and out, you'll cut dusting and vacuuming in half (see page 136).Once your matting is down always *dust first*.

Boo! Hiss! Snarl! Argue! If I dust first, then vacuum, it blows dust on everything I've dusted, says Vera Vacleak, Coal Dust, North Yorkshire. If your vacuum is in that bad a shape you're wasting your time dusting *or* vacuuming. A good vacuum with a decent filter bag and clamps won't leak and spew dust over cleaned surfaces. When you can *see* 'resident dust' (it causes that dusty/burny smell when you turn your vacuum on) as well as smell it, you know your filter's no good. A vacuum has to be maintained. Get rid of that bag at least once a year. (I'm joking of course.) Seriously, if you throw the thing away frequently you'll spend a *little* time emptying instead of a *lot* of time wondering why the vacuum isn't picking up like it used to.

Dusting is more than picking up minute particles of fluff or airborne residue on a picture frame. *Dusting* is scraping dirt and dead flies off window sills; wiping up eraser rubbings and food crumbs that missed the serviette; getting all the ashes, orange and apple seeds, chewing gum wrappers, and fingernail clippings off the living room furniture, as well as the toothpick ends cleverly hidden around the lamp by the easy chair. If you vacuum first, all this ugly debris ends up on your freshly vacuumed carpet. (Ugh!)

I've heard a lot of Vacuum-Firsters argue that even a good clean well-filtered vacuum blows dust and dirt off undusted or forgotten areas onto dusted ones. Well, *get rid* of undusted or forgotten areas – use your imagination. Close in that dusty area, or find a way to rig your duster to get at it.

# How long do other people spend cleaning?

For some strange reason, 'How long (or how much time) do other people spend on cleaning?' is an important question. I suppose perhaps it's really the question: Am I doing more or less than my 'share' of housework?

Ever since 1954 when I began my career in professional housecleaning at the age of eighteen, I've been asked this question, and ever since then I've been collecting information right from the source. I've given talks to over 70,000 homemakers and have asked them to fill out comment slips telling me how long they spend on cleaning. I haven't analyzed all the comments yet, but I have studied a good cross-section of several thousand cards – and found the following:

The women made no distinctions, drew no lines – cooking, dishes, errands, housekeeping, floors, gardens, and the thousand other details that go into running a household all went under 'housework'. Aside from the discouraged, whose reply to the question 'How

much time do you spend on housework?' was '25 hours' or 'not enough' and the many who wrote, 'too much', the calculations seemed to say that it took approximately 3.3 hours per day. (Remember this is an *average* that includes everything from single-person households to families with fourteen kids.) My guess is that it divides more or less fifty-fifty between actual cleaning and the other things like meals, errands, and looking after the children.

Many women moaned about their workload because of a big house. I also collected information on the square footage of the average house and found that one-third of the women responding didn't know how big their houses were – a surprise to me as a builder. Sheer house size is deceptive, because often a small, compact, densely furnished and decorated mobile home, for instance, will take more time to clean than a home three times its size. The age of a home influences how much time is spent, but the number and ages of people using a home ·is the biggest factor determining time spent cleaning.

You might be interested to know that I am now collecting information on the amount of housework performed by spouse and children, and the amount of time the average homemaker donates to civic, church, or other community service. Keep in touch and I will share my findings with you.

Remember that you aren't racing against someone to win honour. What *matters* is how happy you are, and the quality of your relationship with your husband and your kids – not how many hours you spend cleaning or how fast you clean your house. Don't let the speed (or slowness) of other homemakers bother you – unless you are a born competitor, and then I suggest you clean your own house in a flash, start your own housecleaning business (see Chapter Seventeen of *Is There Life After Housework?*), and capitalize on your accomplishments by becoming the fastest professional cleaner in the world.

# Is there a way to deal with 'cow-paths' on a carpet?

I call those unsightly paths angling across your carpet 'cow paths', because they look as bad as the trail left by a herd of cows, one following the other, across a ploughed field. The good news (if it will make you feel any better) is that cow paths happen in the best of homes: they are the result of wear in the traffic patterns of a carpet's use. The bad news is, because of the crushing and matting (and colour change on some carpet), it shows dramatically and everybody notices it.

The logical first step is to buy carpeting in a colour that camouflages the trails (gold, yellow, white, and pink are *not* cow trail-concealing colours). Any solid-colour carpet will show traffic more than a patterned one, and extremely light or dark colours are worse than medium tones. (Medium earth-tone tweed is probably the best.) Sculptured or textured carpets also help hide cow trails.

The second step is to mat your entrances to keep down the amount of dirt tracked into the house. Thirdly, vacuum the traffic areas more carefully and more frequently. If you have a good daily vacuuming routine most dirt accumulates on top of the carpet and is easy to remove.

An inexpensive carpet rake will help rejuvenate crushed pile so it blends in with the rest of the carpet. In some cases a good nylon runner mat will be a dignified solution to the problem.

# Help! How do l get chewing gum out of a carpet?

Go to a janitorial supplier and get an aerosol can of chewing gum remover (freezing fluid type). Spray it onto the chewing gum – this makes it brittle, and it can then be shattered into tiny pieces that will release from the carpet. Gather or vacuum up the pieces before they soften and compound the problem. The remaining residue can be removed with dry-cleaning solvent. If there's still a spot, rub it a little with a clean damp cloth towel wrung out in a mild neutral cleaner solution.

An aerosol can will last a long time and save you hours of distress. Ice cubes or dry ice on most gum will do the same job, but do it slowly and messily.

Because I'm a cleaner and I've seen those nasty little globs cost companies and schools hundreds of thousands of pounds, I've come to feel that chewing gum is ill-mannered. If I caught a person leaving chewing gum in my carpet, I would quickly *remove* the person who deposited it there.

# Don, what's the first thing you notice in someone's home?

I start before I get in, looking for the doormat. If there is none (or only a tiny rubber thing that trumpets the owner's name), I wince and prepare myself for the dirt in the house. I *know* dirt is in there (see page 34), so I don't have to look for any.

The first thing I notice as I *enter* a home is how used and lived in it looks and feels. I'm more impressed by that than by a perfect, expensive, plushily decorated showplace. Is the music out on the piano because it's played – or tucked neatly into a bench with an unused polished seat? I'd rather see a biscuit tin with a few crumbs around it than a gleaming sterile tile worktop. The smell of warm fudge, freshly baked scones or bread, clean laundry, or hobby glue easily beats the aroma of air freshener. Stains from canning fruit on a sink are a plus, not a minus, to me.

I notice wall decorations, too. I like to see family crafts and pictures – a John Van Smear original (if Johnny lives there) impresses me more than a Van Gogh. Dust always looks worse on pretentious store-bought trinkets – miniature ships, dolls and coats of arms – than on family things. Next I listen for the concert of human voices interacting with one another, young, old, and middle-aged – and the harmony of the music it makes.

All of these things I notice before the cleaning details – but have no fear, I do get around to the physical conditions – and in the negative sense that this question is usually asked, I have three top candidates:

Number 1: *Clutter, mess and junk* are a big part of what I notice in a home. I can accept enough dust on the coffee table to write 'welcome', but I can't forget that order costs nothing (and ridding yourself of rubbish and junk can even help you *make* money). Disorder and mindless accumulation not only tarnish the image of a home and its occupants – they give me the unhappy message that the inhabitants are out of control, oppressed by their surroundings rather than served and comforted by them.

Number 2: *Wax build-up* is next. I can't stand dark yellow edges on a floor. It's easy to avoid this (as I explained in *Is There Life After Housework?*) by always remembering to wax heavily on traffic areas and *lightly* under furniture and in corners.

Number 3: *The basic condition of the home* – it pains me to see chipped and peeling paint, walls that reflect abuse and lack of maintenance, not normal wear.

For some reason, cobwebs don't bother me – they can spring up (spin up?) overnight. And dead leaves on plants (on the floor or in the pot) don't bother me either.

P.S. The sad part is, since I've become a 'world famous housecleaner', no one invites me home any more.

# If a house needs a complete cleaning, where should you begin?

I'd start on the areas that go the fastest! Progress and glory are always encouraging (and besides you might get ammonia fatigue and someone else will have to finish what's left). Never start on a bathroom or kitchen – they always look the easiest but take the longest, and if cleaned first always get dirty in the process of cleaning other rooms. My workers were always slower when we started on kitchens, bathrooms, or corners filled with rubbish. Their dirt-killing instinct was dampened and their energy drained for the remaining work. Living rooms and halls are generally the fastest, most motivating areas to commence housecleaning, because they are generally less cluttered with furniture and less dirty. You can whip through them, and because they seem to be a big part of the job, cleaners feel they are on the way to being done, so they really race through the remaining rooms.

As for cleaning order *within* a room, I'd clean ceilings, walls, and woodwork first, and windows, furniture, floors, and carpets last.

Ah . . . but before you start anything, I'd rustle up some help (after folding up the snooker table, removing the TV, and hiding the golf clubs and car keys). Putting an apple pie on to bake is great housecleaning foreplay, a fantastic enthusiasm builder.

# Can I keep chrome looking good?

Chrome is an easy surface to clean, but often looks bad when you've finished. The secret is to use a dry cloth to give it a final polish after you clean it. Most people use either a damp rag or an oily one, and because of chrome's intense reflective quality, every smear is exaggerated. A dry cloth will buff, polish, and brighten the freshly cleaned surface up nicely. I minimize chrome surfaces in my house, but wherever it lurks, use an evaporating water-based window cleaner, such as Windolene Plus, and polish with a dry cloth. If the surface is greasy, clean it first with a solution of ordinary household ammonia.

The way to keep chrome looking good is to keep it dry and dusted, or every little particle and print will show. (If this sounds impossible, it probably is.) It also helps to clean chrome more often than once every six years, so scum and hard water deposits don't have a chance to build up. A little mild acid cleaner will get off any hard water deposits that have accumulated – rinse the surface after cleaning, then rub it till shiny.

# Should I sand my dark old floorboards?

I like those old wooden floors. They look nice and rich and warm, and they *can* be easy to maintain. The yellowing and darkness you see is most likely the build-up of coats of varnish or polish applied to the floor in the past: that old varnish is on there harder and thicker than you think. It will have to come off before you can make the floor look young, fresh, and revitalised. I wouldn't sand it off – it will be a mess and the old varnish will plug your expensive sanding belt, almost instantly rendering it ineffective. And reducing the thickness of the wood, even a little, will weaken the floor's structural strength, reduce durability, and cause it to buckle and squeak. In bygone days it was the custom to sand and refinish the hardwood floor in the school gym every summer. After a few years of sanding, the floor became too thin, started to warp and arch and was hard to maintain.

Instead of sanding off that ugly old darkened finish, buy some paint and varnish remover and, according to directions, apply it generously to the floor. The remover will instantly loosen and 'skim up' the finish to a point where it can be scraped up and removed. If the varnish is many coats thick, you might have to apply another coat of remover in places where it doesn't completely lift off the old finish. (The remover won't hurt the wood.) Let the floor dry and sweep off any dried flaky residue that may remain. I'd then hire a floor machine

with a 'grit' for very fine sanding. When applied to the floor, it smooths the surface, knocking off the old lap edges from previous applications and the rest of the dried varnish and varnish remover. Your floor should be lighter now (unless the original owner stained it). Don't worry about the small nicks and scratches. I know you want it to look like the piano or dressing table top, but it won't because you don't walk on pianos or dressing tables. When the new finish is on, it will look good – or at least, 'antique'. (Some antique floor fanatics beat up their floors on purpose.)

Ask a good local paint shop what the best resinous finish available for your floor is. Follow directions. Make sure you get all the dust and remover off before applying the finish. These finishes are extremely easy to apply. I'd thin the first coat a little (about one cup of thinner per gallon or according to the thinning suggestions on the label) so the finish will penetrate down into the wood; if you don't the finish will hang as a sheet on top of the floor and chip more easily. Apply a generous second coat. Two coats are generally needed for an older floor because age has made it hard, which retards its absorbing powers. After a week or so I'd wax it and treat it like other floors. Keep gravel and other foot traffic debris off it. Use good mats at the entrance of the house (see page 136). And don't roll that piano over it; wheel tracks are one design you don't need.

# How does a 'squirrel' go about de-junking a home after fifty years?

Move. Have a sale, have a fire, donate it to charity, or (if the stuff was already old when you got it) open an antique shop. Don't love anything that can't love you back – that *junk* is robbing you of all kinds of time and energy, and if you aren't using it, what good is it doing you? (It's hardly impressing or benefiting anyone.)

Most junk served its purpose before it was salted away (like shipping boxes, used wrapping paper, defunct wristwatches, old tyres, worn taps, old schoolbooks and 1,000 more shelf-sitters) – you don't *really* need it, do you? De-junking a home, office, shop, etc., will do as much for you mentally as it will to save cleaning time: every piece of junk stashed away or hidden (discreetly or indiscreetly) is also stashed away in your mind and is subconsciously taking a toll on your emotional, spiritual and physical resources. Once discarded, it is discarded from your mind, and you are free from keeping mental tabs on it.

Another burden junk thrusts on us is that we feel obliged to use it whether we need it or not. If we don't use it, then we worry about why we have it at all. Junk will get you – all fifty years of it – don't sit there and argue that it won't.

23

# Are men doing <u>any</u> more housework than they used to?

to school and learn to sew, play a clarinet, dribble a ball, operate a computer, split an atom, identify historical characters and ten thousand other edifying, useful things. But where did you learn to clean? From your mother – and she learnt from her mother, who learnt from her mother, who learnt from her mother, who learnt from her mother (who even made her own soap and underwear). A long time ago it was established that the man hunted, fished, and brought home the food, and the woman gathered wood and cleaned up after all three (wood, food, and man). Along with the tradition of how and what to clean came *who* should clean (the woman), and people are still being taught – by their mothers.

Everyone in the family participates in big Christmas dinners, picnics, potato crisps in front of the TV, welcoming guests or working for the school fair. We *love* it, that's living. But when it's all over, there sits a four-foot stack of dishes that you've done hundreds of times before and will do hundreds more . . . there is the pile of muddy, grass-stained jerseys and tracksuits. The carpet (which you've vacuumed thirty times this month) is strewn with broken crisps – greasy plates everywhere, left lying where they were finished. Forgotten belongings (that you'll have to pack and post on) and dirty sheets and towels greet you after the visitors have said goodbye. Bits of papiermâché, beads, and feathers from fancy-

I'm sorry to tell you it *still* isn't very much. I've collected thousands of comment slips on which I asked, 'How much cleaning is done by spouse and children?' The answers are pathetic. When I was in London recently, a BBC interviewer reinforced my findings. A group of British men was asked how much of the housework they did. Most said 'about fifty per cent'. When the wives of those same men were asked, they doubled over with laughter – five per cent was closer.

It isn't fair, it isn't right, it isn't even *moral* – but cleaning as we know it has generally fallen to the woman's lot and that still seems to be true.

Think for a minute. Where did you – or anybody – learn to clean? You can go

dress costumes are glued to the floor. This is housework – it isn't progressive, only restorative, getting you back to where you started.

Housework is hard work because it receives little (if any) appreciation: all evidence of achievement is washed down the drain or chucked in the dustbin. Where there is no glory, no status, no lasting evidence of achievement, it is only natural to dislike hard, drudging activity. It's not so much the physical work of housework, but the amount of a lifetime spent doing 'invisible' things that embitters people. Doing the same chores over and over again is discouraging. It's accepted that housework always 'has to be done' and 'somebody has to do it' – and we know who that somebody is. Constantly working hard just to be back where you started is not a fair burden to place on one person. This can be changed by reducing the need to clean; planning work out of existence; preventing dirt and junk from entering the house; getting a few good tools that will do the job more efficiently; using a few professional secrets to cut corners – and above all, getting those who 'dirty up' to clean up after themselves. People can learn (before they go out on their own, when they'll *have* to) that housework isn't done by disembodied forces (*someone* has to deal with the stuff they drop in the laundry basket and forget unless it's not ready for football).

Cleaning is everyone's job. Anyone old enough to make a mess is old enough to clean up afterwards. Cleaning is no more a woman's job than anyone else's, and anyone who makes a mother, wife, grandmother or secretary clean up after him (or her) is a thoughtless pig!

P.S. You'll notice that I avoid the word 'housewife' and try to use 'homemaker'. To me homemaker emphasises that the job is creative and that the person doing the work can be male or female. So the answers in this book are addressed to housewives of both sexes – but I am only too aware that far too many of the readers *will* be women.

# How do I get that sticky, greasy muck off the top of the refrigerator?

Dead easy! Spray on an ammonia solution (about ten parts ammonia to one part water) or a solution of heavy-duty all-purpose cleaner (see page 137), leave it for a while to allow the greasy film to break down, then wipe it off. If it rolls off in little balls, it means you've waited too long to clean it and the chemical action of your soap or detergent can't cope with the thickness. Clean it more often and it will wipe off much more easily and more quickly. The stuff is really scummy so use a disposable cloth or paper towel.

# How do I get paint and hard specks off the windows?

I assume you mean dried paint from either brush lap or paint gun overspray. Ninety per cent of window glass is smooth and hard enough to scrape (but be sure not to try to scrape Plexiglass). The scraping system works well on labels or window decorations you wish to remove, as well as on paint. Always use a new blade in a scraper holder – don't use it loose by itself because you'll have less control. Don't use the plastic windscreen scraper you got at the service station – it's fine for scraping frost, etc., but a car windscreen is different from house glass.

Before you start scraping, wet the window with soapy water – this lubricates the razor and helps loosen and release specks from the surface for easy removal. When scraping with the razor blade, *go in one direction only: forward.* Dragging a razor back over the window does nothing to remove anything – but it will trap sand, grit, mortar specks, old hard paint flakes or whatever under the blade and often scratch or damage the glass.

You can dissolve paint with paint removers but this is messy and often gets on the sill (where you don't want the paint removed). But dissolving is the only method for rough-textured windows. Don't leave any slop marks or streaks of remover on the window; they will harden and be almost as hard to get off as the paint was. Wash and squeegee the window when you have finished. (See Chapter 7 of *Is There Life After Housework?*.)

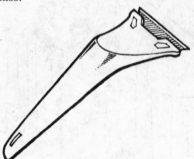

# The routine of housework really slays me - can I break it?

The routine syndrome afflicts almost everyone in every job (school, art, acting, travel, romance, fishing, skiing, and writing can all be as routine as housework). We get up at the same time, eat the same breakfast, drive the same car down the same road past the same scenery. We work in the same place, and although individual situations and the people we have to deal with are different from day to day, we basically do the same thing with them, in the same way. It's hard to get around this, having the same experience fifty times is simply not as fulfilling, interesting, or motivating as having fifty different experiences.

The answer is finding a way to turn your common, routine experiences into uncommon, challenging ones. I think the home offers more opportunity for this than any other work environment. Here's what I do; maybe it will give you some ideas.

1. *Compete* with yourself to cut the time a routine thing takes to do. Even fun jobs are dull and boring if they take forever; the quicker and more cleverly we can do them, the better off we are. (Like trying to find a different, faster route home.) Things (no matter how common) that we do faster and better than anyone else turn us on and leave the routine drags behind.

2. *Eliminate* the routine jobs that weren't necessary in the first place (like ironing socks, folding underwear, setting a

second fork, spraying pine scent, putting on false eyelashes, washing the car twice a week, etc.)

3. *Delegate* – Remember how many now-routine chores were once fun (fetching the post, shopping, buying and sending gifts, polishing, making a special dessert, driving etc.)? Now that you've done them for twenty years the fun has gone long since. You have a family, friends, enterprising neighbours, youth organizations, and professional colleagues, who could enjoy and personally benefit from some of these chores, so let *them* have them. I give most of my routine work away now – and most of the receivers who end up doing it find it challenging and refreshing because it's *new* for them.

4. *Make a change.* We strive for a more comfortable lifestyle – to achieve a state where our lives and emotions will never again feel threatened and we can live in security and ease. Ease, defined, is simply routine, and eventually that's the very thing we end up hating. Environmental changes always bring new experiences, pressures, challenges, relationships, curiosity, risk – and this I promise will solve the routine blues. Try a change in your habits, work surroundings, friends – just remember that the change doesn't have to be *radical* (like leaving home, getting a divorce, hitchhiking around the world, taking a lover, or joining a militant group). I've seen small things like new bedspreads, visitors, taking up a new sport, swapping duties, going back to college, even a new time to get up in the morning, greatly change a routine – and a life.

# How do you clean wastepaper bins?

About once a month or so – after emptying the bins – I take my trusty bathroom spray bottle, squirt a heavy mist of disinfectant cleaner solution on them (inside and out), let them sit for awhile, then wipe them out and rinse them. If tenacious deposits persist, I use my trusty nylon toilet brush.

Many homes now have wicker/cane wastepaper bins. These may need cleaning and many can be washed by submerging in water and scrubbing vigorously. Don't forget to dry them quickly near a central heating radiator or in a well-aired room.

How often a bin should be cleaned depends on the size of your household and the area it is used in. For example, a sewing room wastepaper bin lasts for months; a bathroom container – that has to contend with used dental floss, smeary make-up remover pads, etc. – needs more frequent cleaning. And the kitchen bin – filled with dripping cartons, apple cores, and uneaten scrambled eggs – needs regular attention.

I'm not wild about bin liners (except for the kitchen) because they're expensive, unsightly, and take up storage space. But liners *do* make cleaning easier, if you like using them so much that you're willing to pay for them.

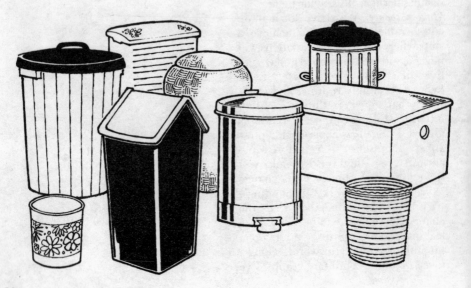

# Is it safe to use ammonia?

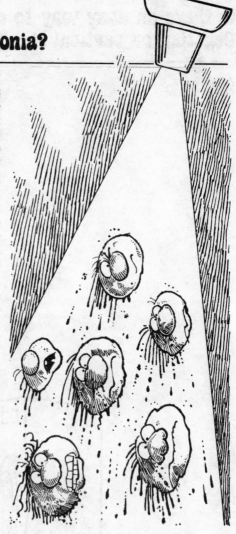

Not very safe for the dirt, that's for sure! That stuff really does stink and it does shrivel up your hands so they look like crinkly crisps. But it also knocks about the dirt, grease, old wax and build-up. I like using ammonia for cleaning because the smell doesn't bother me, it is cheap, does a good job and is easy to find. It is available at some chemists, DIY stores and some supermarkets. Provided you ventilate the room and dilute the ammonia properly (follow the instructions) it will be safe to use. I've read the latest safety reports and used ammonia for twenty-five years and I trust it. However, many people find that the smell of ammonia is repulsive. If it bothers you, don't use it. If you need the power of some alkaline in the suds, use a little concentrated commercial floor stripper (available at janitorial suppliers) in the solution – it doesn't smell and it's good. There are many good cleaners now that have proved to be as effective as ammonia, so these days the need to use ammonia is lessening. As far as the safety of whatever it is you are cleaning, be careful. It does strip wax pretty efficiently, but when used for cleaning the floor in a well-diluted solution it won't hurt much.

# Is there an easy way to clean my Venetian or vertical blind?

The easiest way *is* the best. But before I share my wisdom let me share a bit of history. From the fifties to the mid-sixties, Venetian blinds were a big part of my cleaning routine, at home and commercially. I invented a massive machine that failed, visited car washes (they do a bad job), and tried the bath caper (which most people use). I was always cleaning more of me than the blind. The old cotton glove trick was terribly slow and sloppy. Around 1965 (because no one knew how or wanted to clean them?) blinds seemed to disappear. Between 1967 and 1975 I cleaned or was called to clean not a single louvred shade, so I dismissed it as a forgotten art.

But, like every clothing fashion we struggle with, the Venetian blind came

back in a scaled down version, the mini-blind. But still, because of the horizontal slat design and the fact that they're situated at a window, mini-blinds get dirty fast. Cleaning a slat at a time while the blind is in place is slave labour, and generally does a poor, streaky job. Again, car washes won't clean them well, and if you've tried the bath you'll know that that's neither the easiest nor the best method. For regular maintenance of blinds I'd dry-dust them with a yellow duster or a Vileda duster. By closing the louvres you can dust a flat area instead of cleaning them slat by slat.

After a year or so you'll find your blinds sticky, flyspecked, and coated with a film of dirt. It's time to clean them. *First,* do them all at one time. *Secondly,* adjust the blind so that it's wide-open so the most light can come through, then pull the blind all the way to the top, release the fastener clamps, and remove the blind unit from the window mount. (Make sure you wrap the cords around the blind so they won't drop or get ripped or caught during handling.) Lay the blinds on something soft to avoid scratch marks. Find a hard surface, preferably sloping and preferably outside – such as a concrete driveway or patio – and lay down an old carpet or thick piece of canvas. Open the blinds, hold at the top, and adjust the blind slats to the maximum vertical position (so they lie flat). Take a soft-bristled brush (I always cut an old floor broom in half), dip it in ammonia solution and scrub, getting behind the tapes. The first side will be clean in a few seconds. Reverse the blind (by turning it completely over so the other side of all the cleaned slats is showing), then scrub this side. Use a *little* powdered cleanser (which will have a bleaching and mild abrasive action) on the tapes if they don't look clean. Your padding material (carpet or canvas) will now be saturated with water and cleaning solution and will keep the opposite side moist as well as help clean it. When both sides are clean, carefully hang the blind on a ladder or clothesline (or get someone to hold it) while you rinse it with the hose, shake it once or twice so excess water won't spot it, and leave it to dry. This sounds a little awkward to do but I assure you it isn't. I can clean blinds six times faster this way, leaving them grease and film-free, than by any other method.

Vertical blinds (a modern version of the horizontal-slat Venetian blind) are coming more and more popular. If you have them, clean them like Venetian blinds (it'll help you to remember why Venetian blinds went out of fashion – they're a maintenance nightmare). Vertical blinds don't catch dirt or grease and stay clean longer.

# You say that mats are the most important time-saving investment. Why?

You should use mats *both* inside and outside the entrances to your home. Nearly one hundred per cent of the dirt in your home originates outside; eighty per cent of that comes in on people, stuck to their clothes and their feet. Where is your carpet the dirtiest? Right inside the door, on a three-by-four-feet area where a mat should be. Doesn't it make a lot more sense to shake out or vacuum a mat every day than to chase dirt all around the house?

## Outside

Use the popular Nomad mat which has a rubber back to knock off the heavy residue from the feet and to stop you from treading in rain or snow. Ridged

rubber mats are ideal. Heat or cold won't bother the mats much, and they are easy to maintain. I *wouldn't* advise you to mat the entire step or entrance area. Wall-to-wall exterior step matting looks great, but it's expensive and once the used area 'paths' or wears out the contrast between the worn and new-looking area will be ugly. Cover as much of the length of the main traffic area as you can.

## Inside

Nylon commercial carpet matting with rubber or vinyl backing (see page 136) is best all-round for effectiveness, ease of cleaning, looks, lasting power, and safety (and it comes in a variety of colours). Never use small rugs, or shabby remnants. Mats should be as wide as the door, generally three feet, and should run in length as far as possible without interfering with other furnishings or home surfaces. Many High Street stores stock only tiny mats and you'll have to go to a janitorial supplier.

Remember, the first principle of housecleaning is not to have to do it. Mats can clean more dirt out of your house just lying around than you can dashing around.

# Is there an easier way to clean behind and under heavy furniture?

Areas behind, under, over, are generally non-depreciable surfaces – in other words, dust, grease and grime isn't hurting anything if it stays as long as you can't see or smell it. Of course, knowing the dirt is there (whether it's visible or not) makes it almost immoral not to clean it (plus the problematic fact that those areas can provide excellent rep-

roductive environments for germs, creepy-crawlies, flies, mice and their relatives). And too much of a dust and debris build-up around the belts, motors and pilot lights can be a fire hazard.

*First, use good judgement.* Vacuuming is almost impossible, unless you've got a flat two-foot long 'hypodermic' vacuum attachment. (A word of warning: digging around with metal handles and a damp cloth behind electric appliances can disassociate you from any of your worries, if you cause an electrical short circuit.) Several brush manufacturers make a radiator brush. This is great for getting at the fur and dust: it can go down the side, under, and behind most appliances.

If you must pull an appliance out to clean behind it, remember these items are also heavy and awkward even for husky men or big sons, and one bad drag or pull can gouge a permanent mark in walls, floors, or furniture. Some appliances have short cords or pipe attachments that restrict movement, so don't yank something loose. If you have to pull an appliance out and it has no casters, always lift the front and set the bearing points of the legs on a thick doubled towel or anything else that will slide easily and not mark the floor.

# Is there a miracle way to clean ovens?

Before you begin, don't believe that anything comes off 'easily'. You've probably cleaned more ovens than I have, so you know that everything, including 'miracle overnight soako's', end up as hard dirty work. As a professional cleaner, I've seldom cleaned ovens, cupboards, refrigerators, drawers, or animals in houses, but I've had my fair share in flats. The only magic we found (using the same commercial or home oven cleaners that you do) was *patience*. Bung on your oven cleaner and don't be over-anxious to get to the wiping off stage. Let the solution work even longer than it says on the label. It will almost surely save chiselling, scraping, and grinding. I like nylon scrubbing pads (such as Scotch-Brite) – they whip into the nasty spots around the elements, corners, and cracks.

Make sure that the oven is off before you start. I'd advise you to wear rubber gloves to protect your little fingers from the harsh ingredients in oven cleaners, and remember that oven cleaners will damage tile, linoleum, and other surfaces if allowed to drip or splash and set for a while – be careful. And protect your work area with an old sheet or cover. Don't worry about stains on the racks, as long as the heavy build-ups have been removed. Who looks into your oven anyway?

# How do I remove the stains from the bottom of my bath?

The yellow ('rust') stains you are probably referring to are also found in the bottoms of sinks, showers, and sometimes old toilets. They are generally caused by water dripping or standing for long periods of time. If they've been there for donkey's years, you won't get them out – the minerals in the water have removed the enamel or porcelain finish and have actually permeated the glaze. Harsh cleansers and bleaches and other oxidizers will whittle it away a little, but will leave the area so porous as to stain faster next time. However, a commercial rust remover will often remove the yellow stain – follow the directions on the label.

Any dripping water, of course, must be stopped. Often a 5p tap washer will cure the problem. Showers, baths, sinks, and toilets susceptible to this problem should be brushed more often than usual with a stiff bowl brush to keep minerals from setting up home.

If the stain is just soap scum, a cleaner such as Gumption (obtainable from supermarkets and hardware shops) will take it straight off.

# What about floors that 'keep their shine'?

Most of us know the answer, but still want to believe catchy advertisements more than the evidence of our own eyes. Floor manufacturers claim that the combination of new miracle bond surfaces and depth of material will keep a floor looking good indefinitely. They imply that their floors will keep their shine and never need waxing. These shiny floors are great, but in time, even the best 'no-wax' floor can start to lose its shine. Household traffic can wear down the toughest finish, and detergents can leave a dulling film. These new floors look beautiful and have a very shiny finish, when new, but the 'never-need-to-wax' description is misleading. Sand, grit, particles of broken glass, etc., which adhere to or embed in footwear, will be carried inside and abrade and damage any surface that doesn't have a protective coating. The extra urethane-type finish used on a 'no-wax' floor will perhaps last a little longer than the finish on an ordinary floor, but wear will eventually dull it. Dullness is not only a loss of the reflective finish, it generally means wear is now grinding away on the floor material itself, not just the finish.

A recent study of waxes, polishes and floor finishes by a chemical manufacturers' association ran for eight weeks, simulating the traffic of 80,000 human steps. The study was designed to investigate the claim that no-wax type floors do not need protective maintenance (wax) to retain their original gloss. Findings showed that these floors do have a high original gloss that holds longer than an ordinary vinyl – but that without periodic applications of a protective finish *any* floor dulls, wears, and becomes more difficult to clean.

Many floor dressings are much like whitewashing a fence – they improve the looks, but do little protecting. Instead of 'dressing', keep your floor coated with a good emulsion floor polish, keep heavy coats off the floor edges, and off the areas under the furniture or other little-used places to avoid wax buildup. Wax heavily in heavy traffic areas. Do this and you can accurately rename your 'no-wax' floor a 'no-wear' floor.

# Can you advise about a floor design with hundreds of dirty little indentations?

I think it's the pits! That's like asking me how to clean the ground, because old wax build-up and accumulated gunk are below the surface and there's not much you can do to get it out. Even powerful scrubbing machines glide over these indentations without doing much good. If your cleaner or wax stripper is working properly (commercial strippers are best – see page 137), it will soften and emulsify the contents of the pits so if you mop and rinse with enough water, much of the problem will float out and you can pick it up. But you do have to rely on a dissolving, not a scrubbing, action to get it out.

Two other choices, as long as it's all evenly dark: leave it that way – few people will notice. Or if it *really* demoralises you, replace it – most floors can be replaced pretty cheaply.

P.S. Somebody also ought to replace the flooring manufacturers who are sadistic enough to design dirt traps in a modern floor.

# How do I get black marks off the wall?

Black marks generally fall into the categories of *artwork* (felt-tip markers, crayons, pencils), *club marks* (from broom handles and cricket bats), *rub marks* (from chair backs and furniture too close to the wall), *lean marks* (from things like fishing rods and mops) and *bumps* (from furniture and acts of everyday living – even – gasp – carelessly wielded vacuums).

Don't overestimate the size of a mark and make a headlong dash to remove it at all costs. All too often a tiny black mark on a nice gloss wall causes the homemaker to go into hysterics and –

obeying the latest Helpful Hint book – grab some toothpaste or peanut butter and rub not only the black mark, but the whole general area. Both of these agents do much more than take out black marks. They are abrasives and will leave a large dull spot that's usually more noticeable than the original mark. (Besides, peanut butter is too expensive to use for cleaning.)

So how do you go about getting rid of black marks? First (after you've hidden

all the felt-tip markers), examine the mark and determine if it is removable. Most markers on a good varnished or gloss surface will come off. But remember that felt-tip marker dyes vary so much in their chemical make-up that there is no one magic remover. Sometimes markers stain; sometimes the ink just lies on the surface. If the mark is in a natural untreated wood or other porous surface, it's probably stained and all the rubbing and scrubbing you can manage won't touch it. If it seems to be cleanable, dip a corner of a clean cotton terry cloth (see page 134) into a solution of neutral cleaner, such as diluted washing-up liquid, and rub *the mark only* – not a six-inch-square area. Keep the tip of your finger behind the cloth, the object being not to damage the paint finish or surface. Press harder as you go; this should take most of it off, then buff with a dry part of the cloth. If only a slight shadow remains, I'd leave it. If you think the mark will bother you more than a tiny dull area, dip the wet cloth in a little bit of abrasive cleanser and rub lightly on the exact area of the mark – this will take out the mark and only a little of the surface.

If the spot doesn't appear to be cleanable touch it up with the leftover paint you saved in a baby food jar. Use a little artist's brush and feather the edges out. It will be shiny and stand out like a sore thumb at first, but in a short time it will blend in.

If the problem spot is on wallpaper, glue a piece of paper from your leftover roll over it (slightly larger than the spot and matching up with the pattern). Few people will ever notice it.

When it comes to marks, face the fact that if you have children, grandchildren, or neighbours who are a constant threat, you must provide a wall surface that can be cleaned. Emulsion paint, elaborate fabric wallcovering, wallpaper, unfinished wood and the like are always going to come off badly from a tangle with markers. Egg-shell gloss, plastic laminated panelling, and sealed wood surfaces all resist spot and stain penetration and are much easier to keep looking bright.

41

# How do you clean decorative decor and painted nooks and crannies?

First make sure that it can be washed and that any chips, nicks or damage, cracks etc., won't be damaged by water. Then, (because the dirt, spiders' eggs, and all the dirty stuff, nestled down in the nooks and grooves can't be reached with a cloth, unless you have a toothpick) use a spray bottle and spray a diluted solution of commercial neutral cleaner on the surface. Wait long enough for the liquid and suds to penetrate and 'lift' the dirt, then wipe off whatever is loose. Most of the dirt will be dissolved by the suspending action of the cleaner and float off. I would then respray the surface – again the solution will chemically cut and lift the dirt, which will float off the surface. Wipe with a thick dry towel, as described on page 105-6 of 'Is There Life After Housework?' If a bit of abrasion is needed, work at it with a small soft brush. If it's too old and rambling, what about redecorating, using loads of polyfilla, or even replacing it with some beautiful new wood?

# What are the best clothes to clean in?

That's a good question – clothes do make a difference. You should have seen the cleaners' fashion show at our last conference.

*COLOURS.* Whites are good for one reason: your sense of achievement is magnified because paint or dirt shows and looks like progress. That's why professional painters and cleaners wear whites.

*SHOES.* Plimsolls or rubber-soled shoes are great for climbing around, grip on ladders, etc. Shocks from plugs, appliances, or fixtures are also minimized with rubber or vinyl shoes. And high heels are *out*.

*HANDS.* If you have allergies or super-sensitive skin (or are working with corrosive materials) use rubber gloves. But otherwise it isn't worth having sweaty robot fingers.

Loose, unbinding, *thick* clothes are best. But don't wear clothes that hang down or bag so much that they catch on ladders or corners or other projections. Wear slacks, jeans or dungarees, not shorts – bare arms are OK; bare legs get pinched on ladders, or while kneeling. Long sleeves and shirts left out, not tucked in, keep dirt and falling debris off your body. Wear something you're not afraid to ruin. Don't dress up; people who claim they feel so much better about cleaning while dressed up never get much done. It takes a lot of psychic energy to get dressed to the hilt. Remember, you are *cleaning* (working), not putting yourself on display. You are there to have your *results* admired, not you, so dress accordingly. Remove jewellery, and tie your hair up if it's long and will get in the way. If your glasses fall off easily, hold them on with an elastic fastener around the back.

P.S. Don't go to the other extreme either. Feeling *negative* about yourself isn't going to make the job any easier.

43

# Don, do you help your wife in the house?

Yes. Like many other men who claim authority, I run things around our house...

Said 'things' include, but are not limited to, the following: the vacuum cleaner, dishwasher, lawnmower, window squeegee, toilet plunger, carpet shampooer, paint roller, toaster, taxi service, mop bucket, oven, brooms, sprinkler, hose, dustcloth, etc...

Seriously, though, indoors I shampoo the carpet: wash walls, paint and reorganise; fit, replace and wash mats and light fixtures, act as general handyman, etc.; my wife does most of the routine housecleaning. I also do the outside stuff like knocking down hornets' nests and cleaning the garage.

Although we keep things clean, we use our house hard and don't get excited if a fly dies in a window track. We live fairly simply – I think fancy cooking is a waste of time and over-decorated houses are a pain. I haven't put a single thing in the washing machine or tumble drier for twenty-two years (and I can't work them either).

I do keep the house equipped with good tools, new efficient machines, and the best cleaning chemicals – the material and equipment necessary to minimize housework for all of us. I also bring in professionals from my company when extra help is needed, who seem to do a better job for my wife than they do for 'The Boss's' cleaning company.

# I love cleaning with bleach. Do you?

No way! Basically, bleach isn't a cleaner – it's a powerful oxidizer. Because things have been *whitened* doesn't necessarily mean they have been *cleaned*. Bleach's chemical power encourages its use as a rip-snorting, clean-all, kill-all, restore-all. But it actually isn't much of a cleaner, and is potentially very dangerous if used incorrectly.

Chlorine bleach, used regularly (even diluted), will cause fabrics, chrome, plastic laminates (such as Formica) and many other surfaces to deteriorate. Bleach combined with any acid (such as a toilet bowl cleaner or vinegar) produces deadly chlorine gas, which has ended the career of more than one overeager bathroom cleaner. Add to this the danger of splashing or spilling it on skin, carpeting, clothing, or some other surface, and the injury or expensive damage this could cause. I'd recommend that you leave the bleach with the laundry gear, and use it there – only as directed.

# What are the most loved and most dreaded tasks in a home?

Judging from the calls, letters, and comments I've had from the over 70,000 people (mostly women) who have attended my talks, homemakers are always interested in expressing their feelings on this subject and finding out how others feel about certain household jobs. I've received a lot of comments on favourite and most dreaded housecleaning work, from the comment cards I hand out. After sitting down and adding up the score this is what I've found:

## Favourite:

After turning on the dishwasher, employing a cleaner and completing the day's chores)
The Number One: (almost three times as popular as Number Two) *Vacuuming*.
Number Two: *Dusting and polishing*.
The Number Three: *Washing clothes*.

## Most dreaded:

(This list was much more lengthy and full of pet hates). In the Number One slot we find: *Loos*. The average housewife dreads loos three times as much as she does dishes.
The close second was: *Windows*.
A steady third: *Ovens*.
A close fourth: *Dishes*.

I don't know if these statistics offer any comfort (it might help to know you have company in your hidden housework feelings – both joy and misery love company).

# Any time-saving ideas for knickknack shelves?

Anything full of 'things' (or out of reach) takes longer to clean – that is a fact of housecleaning. If you only keep the things you really love enough to dust and clean regularly, you'll eliminate most of the knickknacks on high shelves. (Maybe the kids can't reach them now, but *you* can't see or appreciate them much either.)

Alas, there is no simple answer to the knickknack question – because there are 2,200,723,857 different fuzzy, prickly, schmaltzy, sparkly, metallic, dull, tatty, glossy, waxy, etc., knickknacks in existence. Many are cheap souvenirs, and they seem prone to damageable surfaces. Even some of the sturdier stuff that won't snag or break easily will often discolour when water touches it, or crumble or fade from cleaning operations. In one house I cleaned after a fire (smoke damage), would you believe I found 7,400 knickknacks? They were of good quality and we hand-washed them in a sink, like dishes. Most good quality ornaments can be treated like this where grease has built up.

Generally, on knickknacks I use a disposable dustcloth that picks up dust and dirt and leaves the surface clean. You could also use a damp cotton cloth. On a rough-textured surface, vacuuming with a brush dusting attachment is hard to beat (as long as you keep a firm grip on the knickknack in question).

The biggest timesaver, if you are a knickknack addict, is to enclose the little charmers so they can be seen and enjoyed without worries about settling kitchen grease, cobwebs, flyspecks and dust. Enclosing usually means a glass cover in front of the shelves – or buy a china cabinet.

A little hard thinking on your part will save a lot of cleaning time. Remember my motto for telling the difference between important and unimportant things: 'Don't love anything that can't love you back.'

# My pet has had accidents on the carpet – can I get rid of the pong?

Getting rid of foul smells is not as simple as the TV aerial bombardment (aerosol perfuming) ads make it sound – as I assume you've discovered. Doing it the TV way is generally a way of masking them – or in plain language, covering up the unpleasant odour with a stronger, more pleasant one. It's fine while company is there, but later the old smell still penetrates your home.

The first logical step is, of course, to get rid of the source of the odour. That means cleaning whatever is causing the stink – pet piddle, dead mice, decayed food or whatever. Shampoo the accident area with disinfectant cleaner solution, rinse, and dry. If the smell is just in the carpet pile, it will come out. But often odours in the form of liquid penetrate the carpet and get in the backing or underlay which is usually made of rubber, so it's difficult to get the smell out. (That's also why cars, couches, etc., that are exposed to tobacco or other smells for weeks remain obnoxious for a long time.) Soaking the area or spot that's causing the odour with a disinfectant cleaner or water-soluble deodorant helps. If the odour has permeated the backing of your carpet your best bet is to replace it.

Circulating air and sunlight have a good neutralizing effect on odours, so don't underestimate the value of a fresh breeze of morning air.

Oxidation (which changes the molecular structure of an odour so we won't smell it) is another method. Bleaching is

a form of oxidation, but it is risky because it can damage fibres or cause colours to fade.

To do a truly effective job you must completely remove the source of the smell by thorough carpet cleaning, followed by disinfectant cleaner. Deodorants and disinfectant cleaners can be obtained from professional carpet cleaners or janitorial supply outlets. Nylon carpets, and others made of synthetic fibres, are less liable to be damaged both by the original incident and by the methods used to remove it.

If you're a dog- or cat-lover and for one reason or another the prospect of endless vigilance against accidents looms before you, I'd advise that you use a soil retardant *before* the problem occurs.

# What do you think of teak oil for wood?

Properly used, Danish oil or teak oil can be of some help in maintaining wood. Like most oils, they are penetrants; they will soak in, condition, and even harden bare wood. This not only helps 'moisten' the wood so it won't dry out, but helps protect it from dampness, stains, etc. These oils don't do much for coated (varnished, painted, shellacked) wood surfaces because they can't easily pass or be absorbed through the membrane coating, and they tend to dry slowly and remain sticky, catching dust. Old furniture, even if it appears shiny, often has invisible cracks that allow the oil to seep in and help condition the wood. If Danish, teak or any oil is overused it will build up just like the aerosol gunk spray polishes (top woodworkers say polishes should be removed each time before applying more).

There is a big fascination for natural unfinished wood today – if you have such a finish that must be 'fed', Danish oil or teak oil is good for the purpose. Personally I wouldn't have furniture that requires constant oiling and feeding or constant polishing. Feeding a family takes enough time and money.

If your wood cleaners haven't cleaned the wood kitchen cupboards it isn't your fault. Danish oil and teak oil aren't cleaners' (Instead, use a grease-dissolving soap or detergent solution.)

# How do I clean velvet?

Velvet wears well, but it needs more maintenance than most furniture covers. Velvets are difficult to clean, and it's generally not a home project. Having them professionally dry-cleaned is the best way to go about it. Cotton velvet and velvet curtains of any description should always be sent to the cleaners – let *them* fight your war. You could shampoo synthetic velvet yourself; the little labels on the furniture should identify the material. If the labels have disappeared, ask a furniture distributor or retailer, or a professional cleaner.

With the exception of crushed synthetic, velvet is not a very practical material to have around. The nap wear exaggerates worn spots. Any velvet (except crushed) will look bad if portions of the nap become matted or lie the wrong way. I use a damp cloth to brush the nap up so it all stands uniformly, but that's time-consuming.

Velvet is easier to enjoy in clothes than in furniture. (Which would you really rather have, a velvet chair to gaze on or a snuggly velvet dress?) Bear this in mind when you're ogling that luxurious velvet settee – and if you must go velvet, remember that whites, yellows, and golds are hard to keep up; browns, reds and greens help minimize problems.

51

# My carpet spots have a horrible habit of reappearing

The return of spots is as frustrating as cutting weeds and having them pop up again. The solution to your carpet spot is the same as the way you keep weeds from reappearing. If you totally remove a weed, it won't return. If you get *all* of the spot out of the carpet, no spot will return. Spots return because of a process known as 'wicking'. Remember how a lamp wick moves paraffin up the wick to burn? Well, when most carpet spots are treated (only on the surface), the spot disappears, it looks good, and the happy spotter leaves. Then moisture helps the stain residue deep in the carpet roots and backing 'wick up' through the fibre – and the carpet looks almost as bad is it did originally.

Any soap or cleaner residue left in the carpet leaves a sticky surface that attracts filth to the carpet; this is another reason 'removed' spots reappear in the same place. Make sure you remove the *whole* stain and *all* the soap residue when you clean up a spot. (See the stain removal steps and specific stain removers in *Is There Life After Housework?*) Remember, even if you can't see it, it's there, so keep working and absorbing and rinsing longer than you think you need to, until your clean absorbing cloth shows no evidence of stain.

# Does Scotchgard pay?

'Scotchgard' is a trade name for a soil retardant used on carpets/rugs or upholstery. 3M also has a soil retardant specifically for carpeting called Carpet Protector. Several companies besides 3M make soil retardants; personally I've had the best results from Scotchgard.

Guarding against penetration of dirt, liquids and stains by using a protective substance generally does pay: Scotchgard does an excellent job on ninety-five per cent of the upholstery fabric I've used it on or seen it used on. It preserves and protects and makes the units look more attractive and wear longer. On carpet I'd make that about seventy-five per cent because people have a tendency to neglect treated surfaces, even though dirt still gets on them.

Scotchgard (or other soil retardants) will pay if:

1. Carpet or upholstery are prepared by thorough cleaning prior to application, preferably when new.
2. It is applied correctly. (Follow the directions meticulously.)
3. The surfaces are maintained afterwards. Too many people think soil retardant-treated surfaces will maintain themselves – they won't have to be cleaned ever again. This mental sanctification often makes the retardant do more harm than good because we stop taking care of that surface altogether.
4. The fabric's manufacturer OKs soil retardant use. And don't forget that a few items have already been protected by the manufacturers.
   And lastly . . .
5. If you hire a professional to do it, get references.

# Is there one single thing I can do to become 'supercleaner' in my family's eyes?

Pick one of your worst housecleaning/housework weeks. Leave town, fall 'sick', volunteer for a conservation project in the country for a week (or die, if necessary), and leave your partner to assume your role and the duties and rewards that go with it. Or let your mother-in-law take control – she'll beat your tribe into shape and they'll never again say, 'Jenny's Mum always...' You'll be perfect by the end of the week.

# Which kind of heating is the cleanest?

The *sun* – you can't beat it. After the sun, you might imagine there's a great difference between electric, gas, hot water, oil, wood, and coal heating – there isn't. Dirty coal fireplaces were blamed for many a grossly dirty house for many a year. But the dirt really wasn't from the

coal (or residue from the coal) – that went up the chimney. More coal dust came in through the door than through the fireplace. Radiant or convection or 'still' heat is a bit cleaner than forced-air heat (whether oil, electric, or gas) – the movement of the circulating air could stir up existing dirt and spread it around a house or room. And of course, we all know that good clean filters make a real difference.

The main reason for most dirty homes in the old coal- and wood-burning days was poor insulation and weatherstripping. Homeowners who put clean electric heat in an old home without re-insulating found to their surprise that their walls got almost as dirty as in the coal days. And those now burning wood (or coal) in newer, well-insulated houses don't have dirty walls. Because of the heat differential, poorly insulated outside walls pull filth to the inside walls.

I'd advise you to insulate well and select the heat that's most economically sound for your area and lifestyle – you'll notice little if any difference in the amount of dirt. Before you blame greasy walls or inside window films on your oil, coal, or gas fire, check the ventilation in your kitchen – the problem is probably more the chips than the heat source.

# Where do you start in a cupboard?

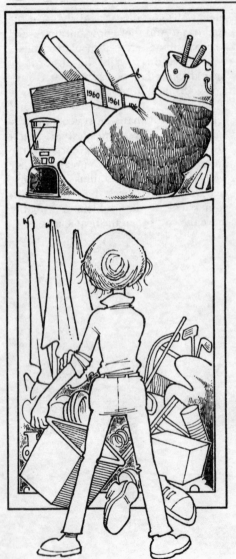

Remember Steptoe and Son? There always used to be a sequence when one of them, would open a cupboard and a thirty-second burst of sound effects and dusty chaos would follow as the crammed-in clobber would pour out. TV viewers loved this because it was so familiar and just like home! The Steptoes never did reform. But you can.

1.  You attack a cupboard by *de-junking* it. That is the simple (and often heart-rending) process of throwing out everything you don't use or need. We all know what *is* junk and what isn't. Dresses, shirts, and shoes that haven't fitted or pleased you for the last twelve years won't ever – ditch them. Those hand-painted ties and leopard-skin handbags aren't coming back into fashion – ditch them. Those boxes of Christmas cards from 1979, 1980, 1981, 1982 complete with address lists: face the fact that you'll never use them ... burn them. Etc, etc.

    That's Principle Number One. DE-JUNK YOUR CUPBOARD.

2.  Move the useful but used-once-a-year (or every two to five years) stuff to a less vital (inactive) storage area. Remember, cupboards are your most accessible (active) storage area. Attics, under the cellar steps, or cellar storage rooms are not, so transfer the worthwhile but not-frequently-used stuff (like camping gear, out-of-season clothes, fencing helmets, suit-

cases etc.) to other areas.

3. *Pick up stuff from the floor.* Mess scattered all over the floor is about the most psychologically devastating of all messes. Most cupboards have a lot of unused upper room – £3 worth of material and a spare hour or two and you can fit (or do a deal with a friend to fit) a second shelf above the one over the hanger rack.

4. If you are a person who rotates shoes, clothes, or gadgets for 'hygiene' or fashion there are pocketed wall or cupboard organizers you'll find useful. Just use your head in choosing – and fitting – them. Some are a great help; and others, just another kind of clutter.

5. I realize most of us don't have enough cupboard space – but try, really try, not to pack too much into yours. You'll defeat the purpose. No matter how cleverly you fit it all in, put it into alphabetical order and organize it – if a system doesn't stand up to quick, convenient use, it's ultimately doomed and will aggravate the mess.

6. Use hard-finish, light-coloured gloss when you paint, so hanger marks can easily be cleaned off.

7. Relax – cupboards don't need to be cleaned like the rest of the house because they are essentially concealed storage, not a public area even to the family, so there is some excuse for having your cupboard any way you like.

# Can you help me with my gungy bathroom joints (grout)?

The typical gungy shower has a build-up of body oils and soap scum, maybe even mildew. I'd clean it first with a detergent that contains *butyl cellusolve* such as Bri-Chem's Super Clean (read the container or ask at a janitorial supplier); this will cut the oils. Then hit it with a mild phosphoric acid (the base of several tile- and grout-cleaning compounds); it's less dangerous to use than harsh acids and does just as well. A mild bleach solution is helpful in killing mildew and whitening stained grout, and it won't damage ceramic tile.

Dirty mortar joints are a universal problem that can be reduced, if not prevented, by some precautionary measures:

1. Always make sure grout is sealed before you use it. Your tile dealer can tell you what you will need and how to apply it. Grout is best sealed when new. Once oils, stains, and moisture have penetrated it, sealing is less effective.
2. Squeegee or wipe down the shower walls after every use.
3. Clean regularly with a disinfectant cleaner, and in the long run you'll spend less time 'grout routing'.
4. If you're building or remodelling, use darker mortar. It looks nice and eventually will help hide the problem.

Avoid miracle bath and shower mortar whiteners – most of them are just more expensive versions of the household bleach solution. And remember that bleach is just an oxidizer, so its results are just temporary.

# Is there a line between 'clean enough' and 'too clean'?

As my Grandma (a mother of fifteen children who always had a clean house) said, 'If the dishes are on the sink ready to do and my husband wants me at that moment to be or go somewhere with him (fun or work), that's clean enough.'

Somewhere between the health hazard, Bertha Buried, and the compulsive cleaner, Annie Septic, is a standard that fits your values, energies, budget, and personal need for cleanliness and order. Decide on the level of cleanliness, order, and hygiene that suits you emotionally, physically, and financially, and stick to it; remember that *you* must be comfortable with the level – double standards never work. That means when May Tickulus comes to your house, you can't quickly get your home looking immaculate, then tolerate an inch of sawdust on the floors the next week when the Boy Scouts are making go-carts.

There is 'clean' dirt and 'dirty' dirt. There's no sin in *making* a mess – all achievement requires a mess of some kind – the sin is in *leaving* the mess. Thousands of chronic cleaners have swept family and friends out of the door because they didn't know when clean was clean enough. And an equal number of grime lovers have achieved the same thing with filth and disorganization.

59

# My white metal cupboards are clean but dull-looking. What can I do?

Many homes have cupboards which were originally painted with white (or other colours) enamel. Because of ageing (mostly caused by cleaning) they don't have their original sheen. If a surface dulls – even a glass surface – it has little reflective value and hence no shine. As enamel cupboards grow dull, they become harder to clean and never look as classy, even if the original coat of paint is still intact. Constant use of powdered cleansers and scouring pads harms them faster than using soft white nylon pads and neutral cleaner solution. Ultraviolet light (sunlight) in time will gradually yellow them. It's purely an aesthetic problem but if lack of shine or a yellowish colour bothers you:

1. Once they are clean, use a silicone furniture polish such as Mr Sheen which will restore the reflection.

2. Replace them – but I wouldn't. Most metal cupboards are strong and straight, and new units (including the cost of removing the old ones and hanging new ones) can work out at £1000 to £5000. Besides, you'll end up with a pile of old cupboards that you'll never throw away 'because they're still in perfect shape' (except for the shine).

3. Have them repainted – don't faint. There is a system now used called electrostatic painting; we paint appliances, office desks, filing cabinets, bookcases – anything metal. It's non-messy and looks and wears much better than conventional hand or spray methods.

Electrostatic painting uses a basic law of electricity: opposites attract. Here's how it works:

The article to be painted is given a negative charge. The paint is given a positive charge and atomized through a special revolving nozzle. The object attracts the paint droplets just as a magnet attracts iron filings, and instead of being sprayed on, the paint is actually *plated* on!

The electrostatic force is so powerful it can actually pull paint around corners. It wraps paint around the object to give a smooth, even coat. Most important, there's no overspray, no fogging or drift, no blasting as with conventional spray guns. It is amazingly neat and clean.

Often, if you just want to do the fronts of your cupboards, you can do the job without emptying your shelves. And if your cupboards have been previously painted, a light sanding will prepare them for the bonding of the electrostatic process.

If you are tired of white, there is a huge colour choice. Look in the Yellow Pages or ask around and you'll locate some companies that do electrostatic painting.

# Can I clean off masking tape?

First, you pull off what will come off (remember, when it's fresh it *all* comes off). If it's been on a while, which is what I assume you're referring to – such as when you tape around a window to stop air leaks or use masking tape to hang a poster – when you try to get it off you'll leave some of the glue and parts of the tape. Acetone or nail polish remover will soften and loosen the glue base so the tape residue can be removed. These removers won't harm glass, baked enamel (such as on refrigerators), or other non-reactive surfaces, but will affect some paint and plastic surfaces if left on too long. Be sure to test in an inconspicuous place before you use it on a surface you're not sure of.

Don't use masking tape any more than you need to. For painting, most people can cut a finer line with a good (slanting tip) sash brush than with the tape's help.

P.S. To hang posters, use tiny nails – they never fail and leave only a minute hole when removed.

# Do you know how I can deal with a dirty acoustic tile ceiling?

You have, as of a few years ago, two good alternatives (to replacement) for acoustic tile ceilings – even walls. My favourite is the dry sponge. A dry sponge is a flat rubber pad that acts as an eraser and actually absorbs dirt from the surface when rubbed across acoustic tiling. It is extremely fast and unmessy. (It is only available from Diswinco – see page 135.)

Acoustic tiles can be easily and permanently damaged beyond most ordinary cleaning means by the combination of oils, grease, cigarette smoke, water leak stains, and the sags and tears that come with time. Eventually, because of the absorbent quality of even a dry sponge won't do much good.

When tiling is in bad shape, the final alternative is to paint it. Painting, of course, will improve the overall appearance and offer a better surface for future cleaning. The bad news is that painting affects the acoustic value (and the acoustics are generally the reason the tile was fitted in the first place); it also clogs up in the cracks and the design or print, sometimes making it look a little tatty.

Because dirty tiling is and has been a big problem in commercial cleaning some people recently worked out a way to 'oxidate' or renew the surface without using paint; we have used this new system successfully in our commercial buildings. Discoloration on acoustic ceilings is of three general types, each of which is removed separately:

1. Dirt and soot – especially around heating and cooling vents.
2. Yellow-brown material – residue and tars from tobacco smoke and cooking fumes.
3. Stains from water soaking through the ceiling.

During the cleaning process, the loosely adhering dirt and soot are removed by brushing and vacuuming. The cleaning solution, which is sprayed on, contains a variety of ingredients, each of which attacks a particular component of the yellow-brown grease and tar residue. The dirt, having had its physical properties changed by the chemical, loosens and dissipates. The cleaning chemical will also loosen dirt on fixtures which can then be wiped down.

A similar approach to this was used a few years ago, with a bleach spray; it did a fairly good job, but the vapour could cause chemical pneumonia and the ceiling smelt like a swimming pool afterwards. If you have a lot of tiling in your house, flat or office, get in touch with Condor Hardware Ltd (Tel: Winchester 63577) who will tell you where you will find your nearest source of cleaning solution and assistance. The new method should be dead easy in a home. Follow directions – and make sure you cover up everything – and you will be impressed. If damaged or stained spots remain, feather over them with a little flat white emulsion paint.

But try the dry sponge first. It's easier.

# Dogs' hair drives me potty. Can you help?

Animal fallout (shedding of hair) on floors, furniture, clothes and inside cars, is a problem many people are stuck with. The best cure is to keep the animal outside. The next best is a good beater brush on your vacuum – hair has little 'lift', so plain attachment tools without a beater brush are slow and ineffective. The revolving brush will help lift the hair or fur from the surface; once detached from the surface of the rug, upholstery, or piece of clothing, it can be vacuumed more effectively. The next move is to get a hand carpet brush with stiff bristles which will gather the loose animal hair to a central spot, so you can dustpan or vacuum it up. Hair doesn't stick to hard-surface floors, walls and furniture, so it can easily be picked up with a dusting cloth. A shag-pile carpet hides hair better than a low-pile one!

Glueing your pet to one spot might also be a good idea.

# What is the best way to clean carpets?

The best carpet cleaner by far is a combination of effective matting to keep dirt out (see page 136) and a good vacuuming every day with a beater bar-equipped machine to remove any dirt that does get in. Eighty per cent of carpet dirt comes in by foot traffic, and good mats at the entrances will keep a great deal of it from ever getting onto the carpeting. Add daily vacuuming with a good beater bar vacuum to your matting, and you will vastly reduce the amount of deep cleaning your carpet will require.

When your carpet does reach the point where it needs to be cleaned, my advice is to have it done by a professional. He will have the equipment and expertise needed to get out all the deeply embedded dirt that damages carpet, and to take care of special stain removal problems. Hire equipment doesn't have the power to do a good job, and most amateurs don't have the know-how or the chemicals they need to achieve a really good deep cleaning on their carpeting.

The best method to ask for is a combination of rotary shampoo on heavily soiled areas and hot water (steam) extraction overall, with pre-spraying where necessary. After your carpet has been cleaned, or when you first have it put down, I would also strongly recommend the application of a good soil retardant (3M's Carpet Protector is one) to help your carpet shed dirt and stains and extend the time between major cleanings. But check before you treat, because some manufacturers treat carpets before they leave the factory. A professionally deep-cleaned and dirt-protected carpet will look nice for a long time with nothing more than the necessary daily maintenance and occasional spot cleaning. (Look under 'Carpet, Curtains, and Upholstery Cleaners' in the Yellow Pages for licensed 3M/Scotchgard applicators.)

If you still insist on getting equipment from the hire shop and doing your own thing, you'll want to know which kind of

shampoo or steam cleaning solution is best, right? There are so many brands available, it would be impossible to list them all, but you can carry out your own simple test. Most of the products do an acceptable job of cleaning, which you can judge for yourself by sight, feel, and smell. The big difference is in the type of residue they leave. Put a little of the shampoo you intend to use in a flat dish and let it dry out thoroughly. Some shampoos will leave a brittle, powdery residue that will vacuum out of your carpet easily and not attract new dirt. Others leave a sticky or gummy residue that coats the carpet fibres and accelerates re-soiling. When a freshly cleaned carpet re-soils quickly, it's most likely because a sticky soap residue was left after cleaning.

Keeping carpets at a high standard of cleanliness is always the way to go – that means don't let them oscillate from perfectly clean to filthy.

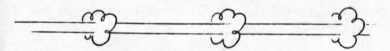

# Please tell me about avoiding serious cleaning accidents

Nobody pays much attention to home accidents until they have one. Then they run around with a swollen eye, acid burns, or trapped fingers and scare everyone with the gory details. More than half of all accidents happen in and around the home; hundreds of thousands of them are directly connected with home cleaning or maintenance, because this is when people use unfamiliar chemicals, climb higher than they usually do, and lift heavier objects. They work when they are tired and get so enthused with 'progress' and getting finished that they forget to watch their step or where they put the paint bucket or where the end of the plank is. I could tell you all sorts of horror stories, but thought a simple visual check list might do a better job of preventing you from having to tell your story of how you survived a ladder fall.

*Overloading electrical circuits is a major cause of fires.*

*Falls account for a high percentage of home accidents. Choosing stuff to stand on is no place to use your imagination — use only approved stepladders and scaffolding.*

*Keep water away from electric wall fittings.*

*Don't leave the bucket at the foot of the ladder.*

*In the mood for a real shocker? Then grab a frayed electrical cord with wet hands.*

*Sloppy storage can be dangerous.*

*Be careful how you store and mix cleaning chemicals — many are caustic and poisonous.*

*Sweep it up — don't pick it up!*

*Don't leave cleaning goodies on the stairs.*

*Get help lifting heavy objects. Next to falls, lifting injuries are the most common.*

*Never reach under a beater-bar vacuum to see if the beater is working.*

*To avoid slips and falls, rubber-soled shoes are the safest to use while cleaning.*

*Don't wring out mops with you hands — they pick up glass, pins, needles, toothpicks, and other sharp objects.*

*Move the bucket before you move the ladder.*

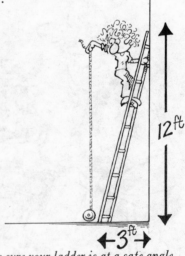

*Make sure your ladder is at a safe angle and firmly anchored. When you use a ladder, angle 1 foot from wall for every 4 feet of height. Never stand on top rung.*

69

# What should I do with my wood surfaces?

*Not* what you've been led to believe! Tons of conditioners, oils, solvent spirits, wood-o-save, wood-luv, grain groomers, and other concoctions are foisted on unsuspecting homemakers as good for wood. Most wood surfaces (walls, panelling, floors, furniture) have a coat or two of a clear resinous finish over them that seals off the actual surface of the wood and presents a varnish or plastic finish – it doesn't allow any of this 'miracle' wood stuff to get to the wood anyway, so you can use the same diluted cleaners on your wood that you use to clean other surfaces.

No special procedure is needed to clean wood that has a sealed finish. I use wax stripper on my pine cupboards – it dissolves the kitchen grease and oil in seconds and doesn't hurt the wood because it doesn't ever *get* to the wood. On panelling, I've always used a diluted solution of a vegetable oil soap. Note, I said *soap* – not because the finish needs to be oiled but because the soap contains enough vegetable oil to make the panels shine up when cleaned and buffed, which saves application of the spray gunk polishes. Harsher cleaners won't promote a nice sheen.

I don't really know how to clean bare wood. If it is smoke-stained, greased, or crayoned, cleaning generally makes it worse. If moisture gets into wood, it swells the grain and accelerates deterioration, and if the wood has paint or finish on it, the swelling will eventually chip off the finish. So it isn't wise to wet your wood down (most of you know that, thus the miracle wood oils are sought). If you want to keep bare or raw wood around (if you *want* to suffer), it may need to have a

penetrating oil applied each time it dries out.

Wood surfaces are nice in a home; they project homely warmth, but when you plan them, make them maintainable. Wood that keeps you so busy cleaning and treating that you don't have time to appreciate it is stupid. (All the knots aren't in the wood.)

I think feeding wood (walls, furniture, or the like) is a ridiculous waste of effort and material. Finishes are available that seal the surface, and if applied correctly form a glass-like membrane over the wood. That beautiful grain will still be bright and clear and fully visible, but marks and stains end up on the membrane instead of in the wood. Use a satin or low-lustre finish, if you want to keep that 'natural' look.

If you wish to apply or reapply a varnish or membrane coat on ailing wood surfaces:

1. First, clean the surface with a strong cleaning solution (a strong ammonia solution, wax stripper, or degreaser if sealed, solvent if raw) to shift all dirt and oils, and so on.
2. Leave it to dry until any swollen wood grain goes down.
3. A few strokes of superfine sandpaper will take care of any bumps.
4. Then wipe with a cloth dampened with paint thinner (or a damp cloth) to pick up any fluff or dust on the surface.
5. Apply the varnish (paying attention to the directions. It may take two coats.

If you have any other questions, consult a good local paint shop.

# Don, do you think it's immoral to have a domestic help?

Sounds like a loaded question. I left this question just as it was asked because deciding to get domestic help is often more of a moral than a financial issue. The question really should have been 'Do you think it's wrong to get someone else to do your cleaning?'

The answer is simple – no. I think it's terrific to get someone else to help around the house, if you need it. We all use professional help with the things we can't, won't, or don't want to do. (Think of transport, making or dry-cleaning clothes, baking our bread, sending flowers, setting our hair, selling our homes, delivering our shopping, teaching our children or fixing our plumbing.) All of these we *could* do ourselves, but for various reasons we find it more intelligent, economical, convenient or satisfying to pay someone else to do it. None of these things – which we delegate without a second thought every day and week of our lives – is any more skilled or personal than waxing floors, shampooing carpet or cleaning high light fixtures. Many people have physical conditions (such as allergies) or emotional hang-ups (fear of heights, noise, spiders, etc.) that make cleaning a horror. Others entertain constantly and have ten times their share of cleaning, or they work a full-time job outside the home. I'm a well-known professional cleaner, yet I get someone else to clean my office because she does it well, has more time than I do and needs a job. So I feel good about it. Getting

professional or outside help *is* the intelligent – 'moral' – even admirable – thing to do.

I'm a professional cleaner; that's what a domestic help is. 'We' do work where/when people can't justify doing it themselves. If you don't really need help, but just have to have someone for the prestige, that's fine, too – it's a lot cheaper than a psychiatrist. We cleaners like to improve the mental as well as the physical quality of a home.

. Once people use professional help they usually find it is much more useful and far less expensive than membership of a health club or twenty extra gadgets in a car. It's totally 'moral' to have domestic help. . .

# Can you tell me any nifty way to make beds?

Yes. Keep the number of blankets and covers you use to the minimum – a couple of thick ones are better than four thin ones that you'll spend half the morning smoothing and straightening out. Buy or make a duvet that serves as a bedspread too, with decorative trim that follows the contours of the bed. Make sure the duvet has a cover that slips off for easy laundering. Don't have excess or over-decorated pillows or valances for fanciness – they end up being a pain in the neck.

If there are several different sizes of beds in the house (king, queen, double, twin, foldaway), have different-coloured linen for each one to save struggling with the wrong sheets on the wrong bed.

Learn how to make a bed so that you only walk around it once; the hotel professionals do it that way (that means don't spread one cover, then circle, tuck, spread, circle, tuck, etc.). Spread all the covers from one side, then circle around, tucking as you go. Make friends with a housekeeper from a large hotel nearby and get him or her to teach you.

# How do I clean bricks?

This question, like many I get about inside masonry surfaces, refers to bare or 'raw' brick. Because the majority of brick surfaces are left untreated or unsealed they can easily be penetrated by stains and marred by abuse. Although masonry surfaces are easy to maintain, you generally have a rough time getting them clean when they *do* need it. To begin with, because brick is so rugged-looking we aren't careful about dirtying it, and then its homely look prompts us to let it go longer than usual before trying to clean it. When we finally face the job, the brick has had years of attack from stains, fire, smoke, insect sprays, sellotape – you name it.

How do you clean it? Your friends have told you to use hydrochloric acid, because that's what professional brick-layers clean up with after a job. *Wrong* – hydrochloric acid isn't a cleaner; brickies use it to wash down a brick surface after building it, because the acid dissolves the binders in the drops of mortar that may have spilled on the bricks during construction. Hydrochloric acid generally leaves a new brick surface looking bright . . . but remember, mortar slop is all that was on it. *Your* brick is embellished with mustard, flyspecks, fireplace smoke, hand lotions, dust, duster fluff, glue, grit that has flaked off, cooking oils, drink spills, etc. – acid won't help with most of those.

Step 1. Brush and vacuum the entire brick surface carefully to pull out every bit of sand or dust.

Step 2. Dry-sponge the entire area (see page 135).

Now it's time to make a critical decision. Every brick/stone masonry wall is different, in what it's made of and the resulting texture and hardness (for example, sandstone is much softer and more porous than slate or granite.) If you have a hard non-porous surface to work with, you can use a diluted ammonia solution and scrubbing brush. If you flood the wall and scrub like a demon, the dirt and gunge will roll off in soapy waves. But if your brick/mortar is soft and porous, the solution might help drive the muck permanently into the surface and you'll have a still-dirty wall with the wet look. That's why it's important to get as much of the loose dirt or film off as possible before you use any liquid that might set the dirt into the brick or mortar. If the brick wall is hard the dirt will float out – then you can absorb it with towels and scrub once more. When the cleaning water starts looking dirty, rinse with clear water and let it run off.

I've also cleaned many brick walls with just a dry sponge; both methods work well.

On fireplaces or brick walls that seem to be beyond any help, you can always sandblast. Sandblasting does a good job of cleaning but later you'll find sand in everything – cornflakes, salt shakers, shoes, clothes, make-up – *everything*. The easiest way is to apply a coat or two of satin (low-sheen) masonry seal *before* a brick or stone wall gets dirty, or after it has been cleaned/restored. Your wall will then present a surface that discourages dirt and is faster and easier to clean. Ask a reputable builder's merchant what low-sheen finish to use, and also ask about any special soft/porous stone or brick problem you are faced with. I always paint or stain my mortar joints once the wall is in place. It's easy to do and looks ten times better than most drab concrete mortar – or attempts at mixing colour *into* the mortar.

On any brick or stone surface, whether you're planning to clean, paint, sandblast, or seal, try a small inconspicuous area first if you have any doubts.

# Can anyone enjoy a real fire with all that grotty soot and ash?

I've had fireplaces in all my homes – in fact, I designed and built them myself, thinking of course that I could always heat my house with them after the enemy had cut off all our oil supplies, and the A-bomb had cut off all electricity. When I learnt that most fireplaces pull heat *out* of the house instead of putting it in, I converted the open hearth to a metal insert (a wood- or coal-burning stove that fits neatly inside the fireplace). I had a warmer house, but still had soot and ashes.

At a recent booksellers' conference I met Dee and David Stoll, well-known professional chimney sweeps. I found out that chimney sweeping is a serious and necessary business: if your heating unit, be it a stove, fireplace, or whatever, is working well, soot and ash will be kept to the minimum. I've seen properly installed round boiler units burn for weeks – they were so efficient only a few handfuls of ash remained.

In time creosote and soot will accumulate in any chimney, greatly reducing its efficiency, increasing the chances of getting dirt and smoke throughout your home, and making you susceptible to a dangerous chimney fire. Clean your chimney, then check the dampers (see that the opening and closing mechanism works). That's the easiest way to get rid of grot. There are many professional chimney sweeps available; however, make sure they know how to inspect as well as to clean. If you are an adept roof scaler and want to do it yourself, you can purchase chimney rods and brushes (they come with directions). Make sure you seal off the bottom or you'll have monstrous black ashes all over your house.

# ... and what about cleaning the fireplace?

When homeowners ask this question, they're usually referring to the exterior brick face of the unit, not the fire grate or ash pan. A fireplace probably has more aesthetic appeal than energy or money-saving value, so those ninety-five per cent of fireplaces with soot-blackened, grimy fronts cause owners not a little discomfort. Unsuccessful attempts to clean these often leave the face looking worse than before, and impossible ever to get clean, so be cautious. (See page 74 on cleaning brick.)

Before you baptize it with gallons of chemicals and liquids, check the surface. If your fireplace is constructed of light, soft sandstone or stark white unsealed brick, moisture will drive stains and dirt deeper into the surface. If the stone is extremely hard and non-porous, then all you need is a bucket of ammonia water or cleaning solution and a good stiff-bristled brush – and go to it. After the grime has all oozed out, spray-rinse with clear water (using a spray bottle) and use some terry towelling to absorb excess water.

If you have a soft, porous surface and a ten-year accumulation of grime, you probably aren't going to get it sparkling clean, because time, humidity, heat, etc., have already become locked in the dirt film. Sometimes it's best to just leave it and call it 'rural'.

My first advice about cleaning any fireplace is to vacuum it with a small hand brush attachment, then go over it with a dry sponge. (See page 135.) If you now think it's washable, scrub away; if not, I'd leave it. Or sandblast it or paint it. Yes, bricks painted with a white egg-shell gloss look bright and can be cleaned easily. Whatever you do, don't try to clean your fireplace with a bricklayer's hydrochloric acid bath (like your 'expert' neighbour suggested). Acid baths are effective on new brick because they break down mortar chemical binders, but on old dirty, greasy, dingy bricks they are relatively helpless. Half-cleaned bricks look worse than uncleaned ones. If mortar joints look bad, I always paint mine with an opaque coloured stain – it is quick to apply and accents the stone or brick nicely.

# What is the fastest, easiest method of cleaning light fixtures?

Before starting, make sure the light is off and cooled. Unscrew mounts or fasteners. This will allow you to take down the shade and put the mounts back on the screws or bolts (nothing is worse than trying to find a tiny lost mount or digging one out of the gooseneck of your sink drain).

Either soak the fixture in a sink of hot soapy water, or wet it down with a sponge of soapy water and leave it on the worktop. (You're letting it soak – just like a frying pan you've left untouched for a few days.) The residue on light fixtures, especially those close to the kitchen, is tough to get off – airborne grease, cooking and cigarette smoke, insects and flyspecks have been baked on by the light bulb's heat. If you have the patience to let the light soak so the sticky stuff will dissolve, the job will be easy. If instead you scrub the unit, your chances of scratching the design or breaking the globe are high. Let it soak until the dirt has been released, then rinse it with hot water and leave it to drip dry. I've seen light fixture instructions that say not to wipe the globe with a cloth because it leaves a static charge that attracts more dirt.

If you need to wash a fluorescent tube take it outside or wear goggles – I've seen too many tubes explode or break above heads when bumped, showering eyes with glass, sodium, and bits of metal.

Lampshades (the bane of the living room cleaner) can easily be cleaned with a dry sponge (see page135). And you can clean any chrome, brass, tin or pewter that may be part of a light unit with a window cleaning solution like Windolene Plus). To restore the metal to its original lustre, you might even use a little metal polish.

P.S. Thank goodness you didn't ask me about chandeliers!

78

# What's the best way to prevent and get rid of cobwebs?

A lightly oil-treated dustmop (available from janitorial suppliers – see page 134) or a damp towel on a broom will pick up cobwebs most efficiently. A web will cling to damp surfaces and can thus be gathered, instead of being knocked loose and allowed to float onto something else.

A well-known pest control expert remarked to me, 'I've never seen a house that was spider- or mouse-proof.' It is almost impossible to keep spiders out. They migrate into the house (generally through holes and crevices) and once in they usually like it. You can spray regularly if you want to spend the money. Or you can seal every crack and tiny hole in your home.

Tackle your cobwebs when fresh, and you'll find it easy and fast. If you let them hang, five coats of grease will settle on them and magnify the problem.

# Do you wash walls before painting?

Only if they need it. The main reason for pre-cleaning is to get paint to bond well to the old surface. Paint won't adhere well to dirt, grease, oils, cobwebs, chewing gum, or sticky foodstuff-laden walls, so most walls should be cleaned in some way before painting.

If the wall is greasy, wash it with a strong ammonia solution. A wall which only shows mild signs of age and wear can be dusted down and painted, or quickly wiped down with a 'dry sponge'. Stains and marks will probably be covered by the paint.

Some things that often do need to be removed are the specks, roller fluff, and hair that got stuck in the last coat of paint. You can't wash *that* off. A quick whish over the surface with fine sandpaper will have an amazing effect on the adherence and looks of the new job. If you are in doubt about some marks, such as felt-tip pen marks, ballpoint pen ink and the like, slap a thin coat of clear shellac over them before painting – it will seal them off.

If cleaning seems impossible with some textures or situations, talk to your trusty paint shop expert – there are special primers and sealers that can deal with just about any kind of surface.

# How long should paintwork last?

Good paint will last for ten to fifteen years inside and five to eight years on the outside. Ninety per cent of premature repainting jobs are caused by damage or desire to have a colour change. Nicks, dents, scratches, stains, blistering and chips are what I call 'damage'. Most of these are caused by everyday wear and tear on the inside. However, the outside trim – door frames and windows – chips, peels and blisters because moisture gets under or into the wood, causing it to swell, which of course makes it difficult for paint to adhere. As a licensed professional paint contractor for over twenty years, I've learnt some rules to make paint last longer:

1. Use expensive, top grade paint. It is 50 per cent cheaper in the long run.
2. Use an undercoat. One coat of undercoat and one coat of finish is superior to four topcoats alone. The undercoat is 'molecular' in structure. It is difficult to penetrate and 'holds' both the surface and the finish coat.
3. Use emulsion paint on exterior or moisture areas. It is flexible and will ride with the expansion or shrinking of the surface. Use enamel or gloss in heavy abuse or 'spotting areas', so grease and dirt can't penetrate. Even

black marks can be removed easily.
4. Cleaning is eighty per cent cheaper and easier than painting – pick good paint and good colours and you'll save time.

Read 'Painting Without Fainting' in 'Is There Life After Housework?'

# Are old or new homes easier to clean?

Modern building codes, engineering, design, and materials put new homes way out in front for ease of cleaning. The average new home has seven-foot-six-inch ceilings; old homes have nine- and ten-footers. Woodwork and skirting boards in new homes are plainly designed with simple bevelling so there aren't many surfaces where dust can collect; in old homes skirting boards are wide and often decorated with mitred grooves and moulding that catch dust and dead flies. Windows in old homes (often shuttered or small-paned) are much more difficult to clean and maintain (and for that matter, to open); a modern house has sliding double-glazed units. Open heat and old-fashioned fireplaces are often thought of as dirtier than modern units, but the real culprit is the lack of insulation in old houses; poorly insulated outside walls make inside walls get filthy faster.

Old homes need old-fashioned furniture to complement them, and while a Georgian mahogany rolltop desk is beautiful and worth £1200, it is a cleaning and maintenance nightmare, compared with a £80 built-in desk in a new home. Hardware is a great time-taker in cleaning; old homes have more. Doors in new homes – pine, hardboard and plywood – are generally flat, smooth, and simple in design; in old homes their embossed or carved decorative trim is a pain to clean *or* revarnish. The walls and woodwork of old homes have usually been painted so often that they look a little dribbly and blotchy, even when clean.

Flooring quality and installation techniques have improved tremendously in the past thirty years; floors in new homes are far less of a cleaning challenge. Man-made fibres in modern carpeting are more easily maintained than the old cottons and wools. Cellars and attics, common in old homes, weren't exactly a help when it came to cleaning efficiency (mainly because they offer uninhibited space for storing junk and cement cellar floors give off continual fine dust unless they're sealed.

Bathroom fixtures in old homes are more durable than the new plastic and fibreglass varieties, but they've stood up to years of grinding, scouring cleaning that has damaged the surface – making cleaning trickier.

All in all new houses are easier and faster to clean and keep clean. And usually, smaller. Of course 'new' is psychologically expected to be cleaner, so you owners of old homes can get away with more.

# What about loo and bathroom carpets?

It stinks! Don't use one. If it's already fitted, pray . . . that your toilet never overflows. The chances are a hundred per cent that a bathroom carpet will receive moisture regularly. When you step out of the bath or shower you drip; the shower splashes over, around, or under the curtain; and the boys have bad aim when they are in a hurry or in the dark. Hair spray settles in (and 'super holds') it. And every toilet overflows one day.

Carpets that get wet regularly are stiff, fade, are ugly and smell musty. They rot. They're a haven for mildew, germ, and insect growth. The next time you stay in a luxury hotel/motel/flat with bathroom carpeting, get down on your knees and sniff – you won't want to walk on it. Bathroom carpeting takes more time to care for than hard-surface flooring and will require more maintenance in the long run. It looks and feels super when new, but it's only new for the first few days – then it's downhill, mate!

If your bathroom carpet is presently in need of a cleaning job, make sure you use a disinfectant cleaner in your shampooing solution, and extract all the moisture you possibly can after rinsing.

# Is there a 'best' way to clean shower curtains?

If you've tried cleaning them in place (generally called the shower wrestling match) or laying them out on the carpet or lawn (generally called stupid), you know that's not the way to go about it. A warm, gentle setting on the washing machine with a little ammonia added to your detergent (to dislodge the soap/mineral build-up) is the wise way to go about it.

There are a few kinds that you can't throw in your washing machine – check the label, or the washing machine after you've finished, and the answer will be clear. Remember that shower curtains are inexpensive, considering the amount of use they get – so consider replacing them when they start looking shabby. Best of all, eliminate your shower curtains (*and* shower doors) like I'm doing in the maintenance-free house I'm building.

# How do you clean an extractor fan?

As daunting as they look, hanging there covered with grease and dust, extractor fans are not difficult to clean. Most of them are removable and – after unplugging – the first thing to do is to unscrew or unstrap the cover grille. Then take it off and immerse it in a sink full of hot water and strong grease solvent (ammonia or wax stripper). Now leave those parts to soak and look up into the fan opening; you'll see a grease-laden motor with a fan blade also heavy with sticky fuzzy grease. This unit is small and light and comes out easily – first reach in and unplug the cord, then lift the unit out of its little motor mount and lay it on some newspaper on the worktop or table. Wipe the heavy grease off with a cloth or heavy paper towelling, then spray it with your squirt bottle of heavy-duty cleaner solution and polish it. (Be careful not to wet the exposed wiring and other electrical parts of the motor.) Get back up on your five-foot stepladder (the ideal size for inside work), wipe out the now unobstructed opening, and spray and polish it, too. (By the way, this is a great safety measure; it goes a long way towards preventing grease fires.)

Put the clean motor and fan unit back in the mount, plug it in, and test it by switching it on; it should work perfectly. Now go to the sink and clean the cover grille that has been soaking; the solution should have released most of the grease, so it will be easy to finish. Dry, polish, and put it back in place.

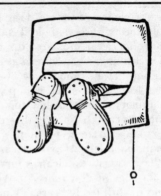

The procedure for cooker hoods is similar, except that in most cases the motors will not be removable. First clean the grille, then replace the grease-trap filter, and if there is also a charcoal filter which needs replacing, replace that, too.

I've cleaned hundreds and hundreds of kitchen fans; believe it or not, they only take ten to fifteen minutes. Try it – you'll be so proud of yourself when you've finished that you'll take the rest of the day off.

# Can I use any old rag?

What a terrible image the word rag has. Rags (old sheets, shredded old T-shirts, discarded underwear, etc.) are a disgrace to use for cleaning. They 'spread as they wipe as they clean' and don't absorb well; they leave streaks and rip up your beautiful finger nails, plus they don't get down into the cracks. Nor can they cope with textured surfaces. From now on rags shall be referred to as cleaning cloths. Use 'rags' to clean your car engine, for flagging down sheep in Welsh lanes and to stuff teddy bears at Christmas. White terry towelling, old or new bath towels, cut into eighteen-inch by eighteen-inch squares, lapped over and sewn once on the long side, make the perfect cleaning cloth. They are easy to use and effective. If they are folded twice, they can be used and then turned wrong side out. This way there will be sixteen soft thick plush cleaning sides which get down in the cracks and texture, protect hands, absorb water and leave no streaks. I'd advise you to read more about cloths in 'Is There Life After Housework?'. If you don't have a copy you are really missing out because it's there that I've set out the major basic housework principles. The use of cleaning cloths, combined with spray bottles is nearly as important as learning to walk and is a cornerstone to efficient housework.

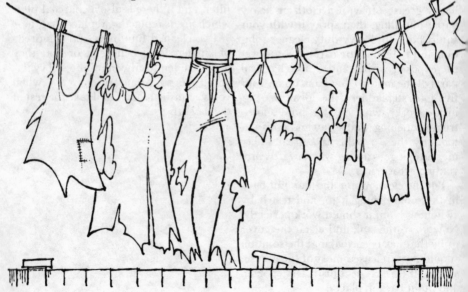

# Is it cheaper to make your own cleaners?

No! You must be joking. All those witches' brews and cleaning concoction recipes you find in books and magazines are desperate fillers of odd bits of space and that's about all they're good for. I'll bet there's not one in a hundred of those folks who merrily recommend that you use dried peach fuzz, ground bacon rind, dried bread crumbs, linseed oil, paraffin, a teaspoon of vinegar and so on, who actually use these themselves. They all go to the supermarket or wherever like everybody else and buy cleaners that are cheaper, better, safer, and easier to use.

It's not your moral money-saving duty to mix your own brew (it is not even paternal or maternal or patriotic). Most people don't dig up their own worms for fishing any more, so why should you feel obliged to pioneer beeswax and barley into home-made furniture polish? I suppose it's a carryover of the 'back-to-nature' tradition – we feel we're being disloyal to our 'home duties' if we don't make *some* of our own domestic needs – clothes, cleaners, bottled jam, etc.

Prepared chemicals, polishes, waxes, and supplies are safer, more convenient, and much cheaper in the long run. Making your own cleaners requires gathering ingredients and additives which are often expensive, and then containers to mix and store them in. You take not only your time but a big risk by combining chemicals that might be physically harmful.

It isn't worth it. Buy concentrated cleaners from a janitorial supply house and mix with water in a spray bottle – that will satisfy any yearnings for having a hand in making your own home brew.

# How about cleaning with paraffin?

The reason many people use paraffin for cleaning is because it's a petroleum distillate and acts as a solvent on many oil-based marks. However, paraffin *itself* is a light oil and leaves an oily residue behind. Besides, unless it's scented it has an unpleasant smell that permeates porous substances – paraffin is undesirable as a cleaner for that reason alone. The inconvenience of finding and storing it is another minus against paraffin as a cleaner. If you need a volatile solvent cleaner for removing oily dirt, I recommend dry-cleaning solvent, turpentine or even paint thinner. Most of the popularity of paraffin is a carry-over from old wives' tales of 1880 when it was the best thing available for some cleaning situations. This is the 1980's.

# What should I dust with?

First, you shouldn't be dusting much. Probably eighty per cent of dust comes in on, and is moved around by, people, so mat your doors (see page 136). I'd also check window frames, clean or change fire grates, and vacuum regularly, and there won't *be* much dust. Secondly, feather dusters, attachments on your vacuum, and oil-soaked rags are out. They create more problems than the original dust – feather dusters and blowers just move the dust around, and oily rags leave a sticky surface to attract and hold dust. Try using Elbie's dustless duster or a Vileda duster (see page 135). Ledges, door tops, beams, wooden shelf tops, etc. are often rough and snag the nap of the cloth, so I'd recommend that you smooth down the areas with a light sanding and a coat of varnish or paint.

The fastest, most effective light dusting in high places is done with a big woollen puff (it looks just like candyfloss on a stick). You can get these at janitorial suppliers. They're called lambswool dusters and are made of synthetic or real lamb's wool.

A cloth, lightly dampened with water, is a good dust collector for the tops of window sills, pelmets or shelves. Remember, your object is to pick up the dust, not to knock it from one place to another, and not to leave an oily film that will attract and hold future dirt and dust.

# My floors go dark under mats and appliances. Why?

It could be old wax yellowing, but it could also be the flooring material itself. Most floor coverings and paints will yellow if kept in the dark for an extended period of time. The ultraviolet rays in normal sunlight (or even artificial light) have a bleaching action and tend to keep white materials white. When kept in the dark, away from this natural whitening action, most flooring materials – even gloss paint – tend to darken and yellow with age. If you've ever removed a picture from a painted wall and found a permanently darkened area behind it, you'll know what I'm talking about.

There is no easy cure for this phenomenon, as this type of yellowing has become a part of the paint or flooring itself and cannot be cleaned off.

Many people don't use floor mats for this reaon. Personally, I *like* the yellowing under mats – it forces you to keep the mats in place, resulting in a longer-lasting floor and a cleaner house. The benefit of matting to you, your floors, and the entire house (see page 136) far outweighs the risk of slight discolouration 'where a mat used to be'.

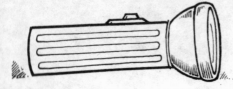

# How do you clean carpeted stairs and carpet edges?

The bad news is that carpet edges – the two inches next to the skirting board or stairs that the vacuum never gets to – are one of the most telltale signs of poor housekeeping. A trained eye will pick it up two seconds inside your front door. The good news is that those dusty edges don't hurt a thing except your ego. Because edges are not exposed to traffic (which means no physical damage to the carpet) the problem is mostly visual. I'd recommend you vacuum the edge with an attachment, not more than once a year. The rest of the time, sweep any visible cobwebs, dirt, or dust away from the skirting boards with a broom or damp towel, then do your usual vacuuming.

Stairs, though a little trickier than ordinary carpet edges, I'd treat the same way. The front, back and side edges of stair carpets receive little or no traffic so dirt doesn't damage them. The step – especially the middle two feet – gets ninety per cent of the abuse, and it's heavy. Once a month or so, get someone to hold the vacuum and quickly take a small nozzle (to concentrate suction) and vacuum the edge. When necessary, I'd take a damp towel, get on my hands and knees, and in about five minutes whip down the stairs removing the fur/dust from the edges. For the middle of the stair, use your beater upright or cylinder vacuum. If it's too heavy to use on the stairs once a week, I'd say it's too heavy to use anywhere in the house. You can purchase a light commercial Vee Kay upright vacuum that will do a super job on all routine household vacuuming and which can be handled easily.

# When is the best time of year to clean?

The best time to clean is a combination of when you feel like it and when things need cleaning. House prouds who clean by habit are wasting time and energy. These are the people who vacuum daily, dust hourly, right on time, sick or well, earthquake or flood – whether it needs it or not.

You should clean:

WHEN – dirt is having a negative effect – appearance-, health-hazard-, or human-relations-wise – and before accumulating dirt and muck and grease makes your house look run-down.

WHEN – you are fresh and well. The great majority of successful, happy homemakers clean in the morning – that should tell you something.

WHEN – every day for a few *minutes* instead of the once-a-week (or month) onslaught.

WHEN – the mess is fresh. The difficulty of cleaning generally multiplies if you procrastinate – not only will it take more work to clean it up later, but it'll be harder to pluck up the courage to get started.

WHEN – you are least likely to have distractions. Interruption is one of the biggest deterrents to cleaning.

Contrary to popular belief, spring is possibly the *worst* time to do your heavy annual housecleaning. This long-standing ritual may have developed because it took the beautiful spring weather to muster enough courage to face wax build-up, cobwebs, and twelve months of accumulated dirt in hard-to-get-at places. But spring is a time to get out and enjoy the fresh earth and air, flowers, and birds – not to be cooped up breathing ammonia fumes and sorting junk.

Autumn, around the middle of October, is the best time (for you and your house) to clean. It's mild outside and the kids are at school; but more

important, dust, damaging dirt, flies, insects, spots, tar, seeds and other debris which enter your home during the spring and summer months should be removed at the end of the summer. If it isn't, it stays around for the next eight months, your house starts looking rundown, you need to spend more time and effort on cleaning, and (believe it or not) you feel emotionally drained. When you clean your house thoroughly in mid-autumn, it will stay and it's cleaner for the holidays at Christmas and New Year. Autumn is also a good time to paint inside and out. Try *autumn cleaning* this year and see the difference it makes.

As for painting, try to select the driest time of year, when there's the least moisture in the air.

P.S. Use mats (see page 136) – about eighty per cent of what you clean up is trodden in by foot.

# Thanks for teaching me to clean big windows. Now what do I do about my jalousies?

I was asked this question by a woman with a heavy accent and not having ever heard small panes called jalousies, I thought that her husband had been looking out of her clean window at another woman and she was asking me to help cope with her jealousy! When five other women immediately joined in about their

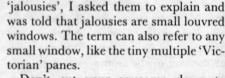

'jalousies', I asked them to explain and was told that jalousies are small louvred windows. The term can also refer to any small window, like the tiny multiple 'Victorian' panes.

Don't cut your squeegee down to midget size and try to use the squeegee method – it isn't worth it and you'll get a pain out of every pane. Bear in mind for starters that these small checked windows are a big window area interrupted by numerous supporting 'sills', and that because of the distraction of the crisscrossing lines they do not show dirt, streaks, or specks like a big unbroken expanse of glass would. Jalousies were designed to give a house a romantic appeal, so if spiders are holding hands in the corners, don't let it worry you, because it all adds to the effect.

I'd use spray window cleaner like Windolene Plus, not glass 'waxes' or polishes. Spray the cleaner on and buff it dry with a soft clean absorbent cloth (paper towels won't hold up long enough for me). The fast evaporation helps clean windows without leaving gunky build-up. If you do leave a streak, it probably won't be noticed, as it would be on a big window. This cleaner will also wipe up the sills nicely after you've done the windows.

(See everyone's favourite part of *Is There Life After Housework?*, Chapter 7, for a full description of cleaning big windows without sweat or streaks.)

# My Formica worktop marks if I dare breathe. Any advice?

Formica is a trade name for a plastic laminate used on walls, worktops, furniture, etc. Several companies make different grades and qualities of worktop laminate, but Formica is tops in my book. Laminates have some outstanding characteristics, including durability, stain resistance, and *permanence*. Once glued down with contact cement they are there to stay. Damage or dissatisfaction with a colour, texture or other characteristic is not always easy to change (a sad surprise to many people). Some colours and textures are absolutely hopeless to keep looking good. And if they're damaged and in heavy use they will become a menace.

Before you start the soul-destroying job of ripping your Formica off, check the small rubber or plastic tips which are fastened to the legs or bottom of the toaster, blender, mixer and other appliances. Often these are the culprits leaving the marks. (If the problem is really bad, you can replace them, but it's probably not worth it.) Treating the points with a sealant helps prevent marking.

Choose you worktop wisely. Textured or matt surface laminates look homely, but mark more easily and are harder to clean than the smooth type. Patterns and designs, flecks, and marbling camouflage marks nicely. Pure white is like wearing a white dress or suit and you know what that's like. Remember, worktops are something you clean every day, one of the most used areas in the home.

P.S. Because today's worktops are ten times better than the linoleums of yesteryear, we often think we can use them as a chopping block, anvil, or hearthstone. Sharp kitchen tools and excessive heat will damage even the best product.

95

# Is there such a thing as a 'clean colour'?

White, of course, is psychologically clean. It has become synonymous with purity and hence we accept – 'the whiter, the cleaner'. Even though white uniforms, walls, furniture, rugs, and vehicles get dirtier faster, because white doesn't hide or disguise dirt or soil, people trust it. Whites and off-whites look terrific in house interiors (walls are one of the most noticeable parts of a home), and can be touched up easily or patched if nail holes or gouges need repairing. Many a handsome home uses off-whites for walls and woodwork and leaves curtains, carpeting, and furniture (rather than coloured walls) to add the colour.

Yellow is a tricky colour to cover when painting walls, and the hardest to make look attractive when you're cleaning upholstery or carpets. Yellow amplifies any darker colour against it (that's why so many signs and book covers use yellow backgrounds). And this includes marks

or dirt. It's a cheerful colour, but when interrupted (which dirt and marks tend to do) you unconsciously dislike it. Yellow and gold carpeting are the nastiest of all to keep looking good after use, even after cleaning. Blue is another colour that's difficult to keep looking good, probably because blues are quiet and restful, so dirt and marks seem more of an intrusion.

Browns and beiges are thought of as earthy or natural colours and hence, dirt and cobwebs, nicks, marks, and fingerprints won't grate on your nerves as much as they would on light golds or blues. In general, pastels and light shades of any colour are hard to maintain, as are extremely dark colours (these even show light dust). Solid colours show more dirt than patterns and textures. If you're *really* interested in hiding dirt, use mid-range tweeds with deep textures on everything you can.

# Please tell me how to clean grease at the back of the cooker?

Those grease bumps grow so hard that even the most powerful dissolver can't work up enough action to loosen them, and they're so slick that most pads, cloths and brushes just slide over them. Use a wirewool scouring pad with a good degreaser (see page 136), such as a heavy-duty cleaner. The little sharp metal edges will easily cut into even the hardest grease, and won't hurt the surface as long as it's wet with cleaning solution. Make sure you let the cleaner soften the grease for a while before you start to scrub – and wash your scourer straight away to get the grease out while it's soft.

# What about those white rings on furniture?

I suggest you drink at the sink – there's no doubt those rings are ugly and difficult to get out. Don't let anyone convince you there is *one* miracle way to go about it. It's complicated because there are at least forty possible combinations of circumstance that could have caused the mark: the furniture material itself, the furniture finish, the polishes or waxes used on that finish, the amount of heat and light (such as the ultraviolet rays of the sun) the finish is exposed to, and so on, as well as the length of time the object has remained on the spot. For example, the heat from a coffee cup resting on certain lacquer tops causes a chemical change in the lacquer, or a cold drink may cause a chemical reaction between the polish and varnish – the result in either case will be a ring mark.

Strangely enough, sometimes if you leave the ring alone, the light and the temperature of the room will cause the surface to heal itself. (A little prayer may help, too.) Light rubbing with pumice, fine wire wool, or a gentle abrasive compound may get rid of it, but that's risky, depending on the finish. Don't rub polished furniture with a dry abrasive or it will dull or scratch the rubbed spot – dampen the area with a little water, oil-based lubricant, etc. (Whatever you use, be careful and go slowly. Woods and finishes vary so much I can't give you a specific method.) If you still have a problem, I'd wash the surface with mild diluted washing-up liquid, dry it with a cloth or towel, and wait a few days. If it doesn't go away try rubbing it with a little furniture polish, or call a local expert...

P.S. When it comes to preventing ring damage, the woodgrain look is as good as the real thing, and much easier to care for.

# How often should you clean curtains?

That's like asking, 'How often should you take a bath?' It all depends on:

1. The kind of curtains you have (fibreglass, lined, sheer, pleated, etc.). Nylon, for instance, doesn't get dirty as quickly as cotton, and textured curtains don't show dirt.
2. Where they are (heavy-use area, etc.).
3. The level of abuse.
4. The professional cleaning facilities available (and their cost).
5. How the curtains look now.
6. How difficult they are to re-hang (and who has to hang them).

The average span for cleaning curtains in a home is every other year, depending on how dusty your neighbourhood is and on the sort of heating you use in your home. If you have older, inexpensive curtains, I'd let them go past tolerable, then replace them. If the level of abuse (sun, moisture, kids, animals) is high and the curtains are of good quality, I'd probably do them every year. Do a visual check and when they're dirty and stained, clean them. Remember, however, that one of the drawbacks of curtains is that they always fade – and fading won't be cured by cleaning. When you select your window coverings, remember the window area is a target for activity. The light draws creepy crawlies, kids, dogs and people. Tinted or smoked glass, vertical blinds, decorative screens and other alternative window coverings might be worth considering. When you buy and hang curtains, keep it simple.

# My mildew drives me mad. Must I move?

Mildew is not a cleaning problem. It grows from fine spores under 'just right' conditions. To move it or beat it, instead of you, just upset the conditions. The three best ways I know are:
1. Provide plenty of ventilation
2. Provide plenty of light
3. When you clean the area of mildew – use a disinfectant cleaner. This really retards the growth of the spores.

Most mildew grows in damp conditions and it grows very poorly in any well-lit or well-ventilated place.

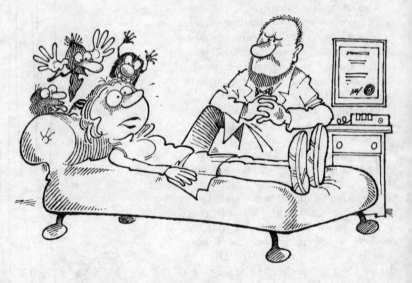

# How do you clean up hair in the bathroom?

Good question. It's asked by 10,000 hotel staff and 788,520 homemakers every day. The good news is that this hairy cleaning chore isn't that awkward. A clean, damp, textured cloth will pick up hair off bath, worktop and sink surfaces easily. The trouble is, the hair on the cloth can then easily get caught or snagged on any rough surface, and as the cloth dries a little the hair will get redistributed on other areas. Using the same cloth to clean the whole bathroom is ineffective and yet it's inefficient to use several cloths.

Professional cleaners and bright housewives can dehair a bathroom in a second. They grab a couple of tissues or a few squares of toilet paper, and dampen them slightly (not to the point of disintegration). Hairs are generally in flow areas of baths, sinks, and worktops, and a few wipes with the damp tissue will remove them. (Don't worry about mini-hairs from shaving: they just flush straight down the sink, and unless your drain is completely clogged up they won't get caught.) Toss that in the wastepaper basket and then proceed with your usual bathroom cleaning.

Here's something else that will help the problem: hang a mirror in an open area away from the sink. This encourages hair care to be practised *away* from the sink. (Hair is less alarming on the floor or mat because a vacuum beater bar can deal with it.) Have you ever pulled out the drain stopper or looked down the plug hole in your sink or bath? Then you won't have to wonder why water goes down the sink so slowly – the stopper will be absolutely hanging with matted hair and soap gunk. Stoppers and plug holes should be cleaned every month. There's no magic tool – it's a quick finger job.

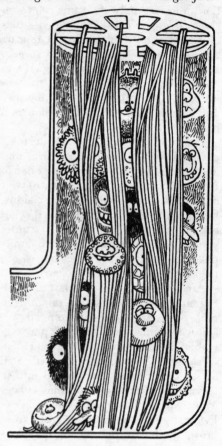

# Can you tell a woman's relationship with her husband by looking in her fridge?

How is it that everyone in the world heard me make the statement that you could? But everything said in jest – or parable – has meaning, so here goes . . .

I'm a firm believer in a principle called *carry-over*. In plainer words, the personal characteristics you exhibit in any situation are essentially the same ones you show in other, totally unrelated situations. A person who's sloppy in appearance will generally be sloppy in speech, keeping promises and gardening. If you are an aggressive competitor on the tennis court, you will generally be that way at PTA meetings, when bottling jam, and in your style of dress.

Your refrigerator is probably the most personal of all your furniture and appliances – behind its door (and often in front of it) is a composite picture of your organization, judgement, decisions, hopes, failures and successes. It's not open to the world (Remember how upset you are when anyone outside the family pokes around in your fridge?) but *you* can tell a lot by taking a hard look in it.

Are you the type who lets the refrigerator go and go and go, cramming in more and more and finally going to two-storey stacking, ignoring spills and vegetables that have shrivelled beyond identification – then suddenly in a dedicated attack of repentance you whip into it, leaving it gleaming and immaculate? You are probably also letting marriage or living strains and irritations grow, grow, grow, until they become intolerable –

then in a big weeping, soul-cleansing trauma, you sweep your cowering family into a confrontation, followed by a tearful kissy-pie all-is-well. But then you start stacking the fridge again, putting lids on the problems that you'd rather delay taking decisions on. You do this until the fridge (or family situation) stinks and is ready to explode – and then you dive in again and make peace, love, apologies, promises, etc.

Those who keep their refrigerators bare (I mean not a morsel to snack on – not a saucer of cold peaches or a peeled boiled egg in there) often have empty, cold relationships with family and associates.

The person who can't manage to put a lid on a smelly container in the refrigerator probably can't keep the lid on a neighbourhood secret.

If you have disguised or hidden 'no-nos' (fattening chocolates) stashed in secret places in your fridge, you'll probably have other hidden things (gifts, rash purchases, damaged things, spare money) the rest of the family doesn't know about.

If a fridge is dominated by processed foodstuffs, it generally signifies that the time the family spends together is limited.

If the fridge is dominated by the husband's 'pastime' residue (liquor, fish bait, film), that generally means the woman of the house is far from liberated (equal).

Before any of you gentlemen and children sit back and feel too smug, the same diagnoses can be made from a man's toolbox, a child's locker at school, scout rucksacks, etc.

# I have four boys who miss the toilet – any advice?

Keep out of the way. Painting a red dot as a target near the bottom at the back of the toilet bowl will present an irresistible challenge. Signs that help create a hero-identification situation also help dry up careless behaviour. And making them clean up their own mess with disinfectant cleaner solution – make sure they get around the base of the toilet and floor area – will improve accuracy by seventy per cent.

Try these tactics and treat them kindly and they will 'aim to please'.

# Any advice on cleaning a telephone?

The doorknob is the dirtiest thing in a house, but the telephone has to be running a strong second in the filth finals. An assortment of dirty (and often oily) ears, hands, mouths and cheeks are in close germ-spreading communication with a phone every day – so use a diluted disinfectant cleaner solution in a plastic spray bottle when you clean the phone, which should be often. A phone in a home should be cleaned at least monthly, and weekly – not weakly – in a commercial building.

Spray the receiver from the top and side – never directly into the transmitter holes in front because the moisture might cause a malfunction – then wipe the entire handpiece with a dry cloth. Spray the base unit and dial and dry and polish with a soft clean cloth.

# Which cleaner is best?

First, don't lose too much sleep over this question. There isn't enough difference in most cleaners to really matter. Rip, Snort, Sizzle, and Guzzle are all essentially similar. The basic elements in most cleaners are *alkalis* (such as caustic soda, lye, soda ash, baking soda), *phosphates* (such as trisodium phosphate and pyro wetting agents), and *sulphates* (such as anionic sodium salts). Different manufacturers use modified phosphate-free or other special material, but this must be balanced with yet other ingredients in order to do a good job of cleaning – and all the formulas end up very much alike. Most cleaners are a sick yellow-brown colour when formulated – they usually have a dye added to differentiate them from Brand X and to make them look appealing.

Consumers are brand fanatics, hypnotized by the colours and jingles and bursting soap bubbles of TV commercials. If I said get El Snort cleaner and a woman couldn't get that brand conveniently, she would climb Everest to find it. We all have strong feelings about our favourites but most of us couldn't tell one from the other if they weren't named and packaged differently.

On most products, if you get the right *type*, you're OK as most soaps, heavy-duty cleaners, all-purpose cleaners, are so similar few of us could distinguish one from another. Concentrated disinfectant cleaner is a type of product of which many brands are available, all very much

alike in chemical composition. Some work a little better than others, but it's not worth the time or emotional strain to find the perfect one.

If you want to make life simpler, I'd advise you to have only three types of cleaners:
1. A *heavy-duty neutral all-purpose cleaner*. "Neutral" means a central or neutral pH factor between the 0-7 pH of acids and the 7-14 pH of alkalis. (See the equipment chart on page 137.)
2. A *disinfectant cleaner*. A quaternary disinfectant cleaner used primarily for toilets and other areas where germs and bad odours are found.
3. A *window cleaner* (see *Is There Life After Housework?*) This can also polish chrome or other 'bright' objects.

I'd buy the neutral and disinfectant cleaners in concentrated form at a janitorial supplier (see page 137) in plastic containers. Buy three one- or two-pint trigger spray bottles and use your own water and the *right* amount of concentrate (not 'a little extra to be sure it works well'). If you buy from a reputable place the cleaner will be as good as or even better than the supermarket variety and seventy-five per cent cheaper.

We'll see the day when you'll be able to bring a six-month supply of cleaners home in a handbag. A great percentage of what you carry out of the supermarket is water; it costs plenty to package, transport and store water.

Products and compounds are not

magic, only your tools for the application of intelligent cleaning techniques. I use a few brand names – like 3M, for example – they produce good stuff. It's expensive, but lasts and works better than most of the competitors' similar products, I also like Ettore/Steccone squeegees, which I don't think can be matched, although other brands work. For example, there are at least thirty good 35mm cameras on the market. If I took thirty pictures, one from each camera, the average person couldn't tell the £60 from the £500 product. So it is with cleaning products – be true to types, not brands.

# How do I care for stonework and quarry tiles?

Stone, brick, ceramic, quarry and various tiles are extremely durable flooring materials and will keep up their looks with the minimum of care. To illustrate my point, I'll ask you to recall the stone floor found in the large shopping precincts you've undoubtedly patronized. Did the floor look dull, dry and scuffed? Probably not. In most shopping precincts, the floors are kept clean and glowing to present a positive image to the customers. The owners, expecting thousands of people a day to be walking up and down the broad thoroughfares, choose flooring noted for its durability and ease of maintenance. When you compare the traffic there with that at the entrance to your home (thirty or forty per

day, maybe) there's no reason your floor can't look bright and shiny all the time.

You can keep stone floors looking either rustic or highly polished. Some stone or tile *has* to have a varnish applied to its naturally dull or porous surface. The proper finish not only seals and smooths out the surface, it also deepens and brings out the natural colours and beauty of the stone or tile. If you have a problem tile or stone entrance, most likely the problem lies in your choice of finish, products and their application. Many people believing the 'you'll never-need-to-polish-again' sales message make the mistake of putting a varnish-type finish on their floors, and expect it to last forever. The finish looks super for a while, but eventually ends up chipping and scabbing like a sunburned back. The secret lies in putting down a permanent, penetrating sealer, topped with a renewable finish material (to *keep* it looking good).

The sealer can be of the easy-to-use water emulsion type or a resinous product, but in any case it should be a *penetrating* sealer. You want your sealer to penetrate and seal – not leave a thick film on top of the stone. Sealers are very hard and brittle, and if you have a thick layer of sealer on top of your stone, it will tend to chip off and peel just like the varnish does. After proper sealing, apply several coats of a good floor polish to protect the base coat and to give the desired smoothness and gloss. This can be a liquid acrylic finish like you use on your vinyl floors or a paste wax polish. These waxes and other finishes are softer than the sealer and thus should not chip or peel. They will wear off, though. The protective coat must be renewed from time to time to maintain its beauty and should not be allowed to wear down to the seal coat. The polish can be stripped off and reapplied without removing the sealer.

After your entrance has been properly finished and is looking good, don't forget to put down a good entrance mat (see page 136) to protect the heavy traffic portion just inside the door, and to knock the grit off. These mats are now available in nice earth tones and colours to enhance the beauty of your natural stone or tile floor.

# Is there a way to keep my mops clean?

Too many people have been convinced that water is all that's needed to clean the modern floor. Well, dirt is not modern, it's the same old thing and needs a cleaner to dissolve and release it from whatever it's clinging to (in this case, the floor and the mop). Use a little all-purpose neutral cleaner in your cleaning water, and you'll have a cleaner floor and mop.

Dirt has a tendency to stick to surfaces, especially to a cloth or sponge. Unless you use soap or detergent to release the dirt so it can be rinsed out, your tool will remain soiled. Using a good cleaner will not only keep your mop clean, it will work miracles on your floor. When your mop stays dirty it's a good indication that your floor or other surface is also dirty.

Many people try to bleach their mops clean. This isn't very clever – bleach is a harsh oxidizer and will reduce the life of the tool. Of course, a sponge mop won't look brand new after being used, so don't worry about a slight discolouration.

# Is it practical to own carpet shampooing equipment?

Almost never. Many people who own or rent a 3,000-square foot carpeted house or flat imagine they are in the big time and need to own their own carpet-cleaning equipment. It looks practical on paper, because shampooing five thousand feet of carpet (at 1983 prices, 6p per square foot) is £300 annually. For £495 to £950 you could get your own hot water extractor unit, which would last for years.

You'll be sorry if you take the step.

1. With good matting (see page 136) you won't have to shampoo annually – maybe once every three to five years.

2. All this equipment (unit, hose, cord, spotting kits and so on) will take up masses of storage area.

3. Carpet extraction equipment needs a lot of maintenance – it breaks down and gets out of tune easily, and will rapidly go downhill if not used and serviced regularly (and we aren't a service society any more).

4. Every neighbour, relative, friend, and even carpet cleaner will find out that you have the equipment and not only expect to borrow it, but feel slighted if you don't accompany it and do the job. (Borrowers are the true kiss of death to good carpet equipment.)

5. The carpet-cleaning chemical costs a lot and has to be picked up and stored.

6. There is the work. The equipment looks impressive and will do wonderful things, but running and lifting carpet equipment (and heaving furniture around) is back-breaking, skilled work – it requires not only a strong back but knowledge of colour, fabric, moisture control, spotting, etc. That's why *I* don't own my own shampooer (and, as a professional, I could get it wholesale).

# My stainless steel sink and appliances never look good. Can you help?

*First:* Don't get overly excited, and stop swearing that you're going to paint all the stainless steel in your house! Stainless steel, especially the brushed surface found on most sinks or kitchen appliances, will tarnish fast, cloud, streak, and water-spot, and slowly take on a permanent 'used' look. In other words, it stains. In some of the commercial buildings I clean I have six hundred stainless steel drinking fountains to clean up after the public. They are a very tricky item, hard to clean – and once clean, they deteriorate quickly.

There are dozens of stainless steel cleaners and polishes on the market, most of which offer only a little help. A lot of elbow grease will leave the unit in pretty good nick. But generally after a dribble of anything on it, the glowing surface looks the same as before you started.

I personally wouldn't *have* stainless steel, even a high-reflecting stainless. Get vitreous china or porcelain fixtures for easier cleaning.

If you do have stainless steel:

1. Clean it thoroughly with a mild detergent solution, (like washing-up liquid), rinse, and buff it dry with a cloth or towel.

2. Some house-proud people treat stainless steel appliance panels etc., with waxes, silicone-type materials, or other protectors for a nice lustre or glow. It looks good, but remember, in the long run any treated surface will require more upkeep.

3. Some commercial aerosol stainless steel cleaner/polish formulas work well (3M is one of the good ones).

It might make you feel better to realise that stain*less* steel isn't *non-staining* steel – it stains *less* than plain old steel, but it does stain and it's not your fault.

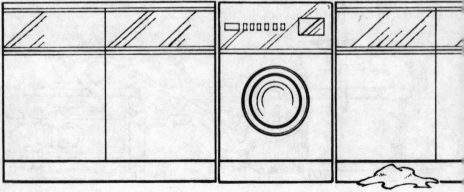

# ... and is aluminium always so ugly?

Be satisfied with aluminium: it doesn't rust, fade, scale, scab, chip or rot. It might oxidize a little (that cloudy grey film on the surface) but it still looks OK without much maintenance. Most aluminium, whether on inside or outside fixtures (especially window fittings), is burnished (brushed) – not shiny and smooth – and is not intended to look spit-polished all the time.

But if the oxidation becomes intolerable to you, mix up any good cleaning solution, rub it on, and wipe it dry. This won't change the appearance of the aluminium much, but there'll be a lot of black marks on your rag, psychologically creating the impression that the aluminium is now clean – and you'll live happily ever after.

113

# My fibreglass shower is impossible. Can it be cleaned?

Fibreglass is now being used to make inexpensive, lightweight shower enclosures and shower doors. Builders often use these units because they are less costly than conventional porcelain or ceramic tile units, and because they are easier to install. Unfortunately, fibreglass generally requires more maintenance than the glazed finishes it replaces, and is more easily damaged. With proper care, however, it can look good and be quite serviceable.

The basic thing to remember about fibreglass is to avoid damaging it, thereby making it more difficult to clean.

Don't use abrasive cleansers or scouring pads, as these will roughen the surface and make dirt cling more tenaciously. Strong oxidizers such as bleach, harsh acids and extremely volatile solvents can also damage the finish. If your soap scum problem can't be eliminated by regular cleaning with a disinfectant cleaner (which it should be able to), I recommend that you wax the unit when new, or clean your old one up, wax it, and keep it waxed to ease cleaning. Products containing silicone should not be used on the floor unless you want to practise skiing in your shower. Most car paste waxes can be used on the floor of shower units without making them slippery, but try any wax you intend to use on the walls first.

If you clean your fibreglass shower weekly, a mild neutral disinfectant cleaner should do the trick and a blue/white nylon scrubbing sponge can be used without scratching. (See the Equipment Chart on page 136.) For heavy soap scum, a mild organic acid cleaner such as Ataka (obtainable from Boots) is OK. If you have a fibreglass unit that has been scoured and scratched, car rubbing compound will polish it up again, and a good wax job should make it look like new. The secret is to keep it maintained and don't let the soap scum build up so much that it becomes a major operation.

# ... and the tracks of patio doors, medicine cabinets, etc.?

Any door mounted on a base (bottom) track will someday cause a problem. The wear of rollers and tracks is accelerated by dirt and the build-up from water running down the windows and doors. Moisture turns the accumulated dirt into a gummy residue that 'freezes' or clogs up rollers when the residue gets hard. The secret is simple – clean and maintain tracks *regularly*. That means don't wait until the doors are beginning to stick; vacuuming them then does little good because anything loose is quickly ground into gummy stuff. Take a spray bottle of all-purpose cleaner solution (see page 137), squirt all over and inside the track and rollers, and leave it to set to dissolve hard gummy globs. Then wrap a screwdriver with a terrycloth or similar rag and wipe out the gunk. (The cloth must

have some body to it – silk, thin cotton, or linen rags work poorly for this purpose.) It's a little awkward, but a couple of wipes and the track will become clean. If the track is kept clean, the roller stays clean and operable.

I wouldn't lubricate tracks with graphite, petroleum jelly, or oil because this will increase gunk build-up. In general, I'd advise two things:

1. Get top roller tracks instead of bottom tracks if you have a choice next time – and buy the best you can.
2. Keep them clean.

# What is the worst time-waster in the home?

*Picking up clobber!* Some homemakers are almost full-time clobber picker-uppers. This is not a rewarding job, because after you've done it you're right where you should have been when you started. Solving the clobber problem does more than free your time: it's fantastic in relieving tension, because you're spared the constant worry, 'If someone drops in now, what would they think of me?'

Another big liability of clobber is that it causes time-consuming fights and frustration. When family members can't find their far-flung paraphernalia – even if they lost them themselves – everyone else has to take the blame as the seekers whine and stomp through the house trying to locate the article they should have put away in the first place. Clobber and clutter causes more arguments than anything except money.

An untidy house is a worse visual and emotional offender than a dirty house because dirt has some natural authority, an excuse for being there. Dirt can be accepted to a degree: things get dirty with use, but clobber is just personal possessions out of control.

Clobber has three general causes:
1. Your family owns too much junk (excess toys, towels, trinkets, ties, playthings, furniture, books).
2. Your home has inadequate or inefficient storage spaces – racks, shelves, cupboards, hooks, towel rails, and toy boxes.
3. You have accepted the role of 'family dogsbody' to a thoughtless bunch of litterbugs.

You are clever enough to cure all three: if you do, you'll cut the time you spend – unbelievably – and the hurtful anxieties of keeping clobber under control.

# Does professional cleaning cost the earth?

That depends on whether you own Dracula's castle, a caravan, a semi, a flat or a bedsit. It also depends on what you define as 'cleaned'. I can give you a rough estimate for the two categories based on prices at the time we went to press. (Right now a domestic help earns just under £2 an hour.)

## *Cleaned by a domestic help*

Ordinary vacuuming, dusting, polishing, spot cleaning, sweeping – mopping, wax touch up – bathroom cleaning, watering plants, etc.:

Large Home ........ £25-£40 per time
Average Home ...... £15-£25 per time
Tiny Home ....... £7.50-£15 per time
(if the cleaner uses his or her own equipment, add £3 per visit)

## *Cleaned by a professional cleaning firm*

When a cleaning crew goes through the entire home washing all walls, windows, and woodwork, waxing floors, shampooing carpet and upholstery:

5,000 sq.ft. Very Big Home ..... £550
4,000 sq.ft. Big Home .......... £500
1,800 sq.ft. Average Home ...... £300
1,100 sq.ft. Small Home ........ £200
800 sq.ft. Average Flat ........ £150

Average local travel costs and preparation time are included in these costs. Remember that these figures are rough guidelines only – estimates can range quite widely – and you should always get references to make sure you're dealing with a reputable firm.

## *Factors to bear in mind*

The state of the local labour market, age of the home and its general condition, type of furnishings, wall and floor coverings, number of knickknacks, etc., make a difference. Location makes a *big* difference. An average-size home on a remote tip of the Cornish coast would probably cost more (considering travel time and vehicle use) than a big home in a Midlands city. Stormy weather conditions, city smog and other environmental factors influence the cost, too.

# How can I develop a positive attitude to housework?

First of all (and best of all I might add) is to realize that it is not *your* housework. Housework belongs to everyone. I've found in the years I've spent doing housework and gathering information that about ninety per cent of the mess in a house is made by children, friends and husbands, and that about ninety per cent of the cleaning-up is done by the mother. This is the worst crime in the world. Anyone old enough to make a mess is old enough to clean up and should be taught and be expected to do so. If you simply make people take care of their own messes, you won't believe how positive your attitude towards cleaning will be. Secondly, any housework you do well enhances the quality of life through the responsibility that goes with it. For a start, it's good exercise (which we all need), and any constructive change for the better in our environment generally carries over into a change for the better in our lives.

I knew a toilet-cleaner who turned his smelly, lowly task into the most rewarding admired job on the whole fashionable ski-resort where he worked. He not only cleaned toilets quickly and well, he also told toilet jokes, wore a zippy uniform and 'bowl patrol' badge and was admired by all the rich and famous skiers because he skied better than anyone – with his mops swinging high above his head. He *always* had a big grin and cheerful word to say. For me he proved that no matter how much you own in this world,

what your politics, strengths or weaknesses . . . if you don't have the right attitude about what you want to do, have to do or simply land up doing, you aren't going to make much of an impression on anybody or anything. Attitude doesn't come from circumstances, luck, assignment, heredity or injustices . . . it all comes from *you*.

One of the first steps is getting on top of, and being proud of, the improvements in your achievements. Personally, I'm proud of my work because I do it well. I would rather do housework than ski, play golf, hunt, fish, play darts or eat! Does that help your attitude at all?

118

# Now tell me about TV's and stereos

Dust is sound equipment's worst enemy, and amplifiers and other high-current components attract it because they are electrically charged.

Dust damages tape heads, needles and cartridges.

I use a dry disposable dusting cloth eighty per cent of the time. This should take care of the surface dust. Remember to keep the cover on your turntable. Periodic vacuuming of ventilation louvres and foam or mesh speaker grilles will keep your components looking good – and operating smoothly.

When you must clean off the hand oils, smudges, and spots on your TV screen or other appliances, a cloth dampened with a mild neutral cleaner, like washing-up liquid, followed with a dry towel buffing is best. I'd keep spray polishes and cleaners away from any set I cared for if I were you. And don't forget to unplug them while you clean.

119

# What do I do about the garage?

It doesn't cost much (in fact *less*) to be clean. For example, three eight-foot two by twelves and a few breeze blocks can offer order, safety, and convenience in the form of instant garage storage shelves. Go into your garage and look around. Here are a few ideas that will help you:

1. Store anything light by hanging it as high as reachably possible. This keeps it out of the 'stumbling over' path, yet readily accessible.

2. Find, buy, or make a wall cabinet (six feet tall if possible) to store small hand tools, paint and lawn chemicals, etc. Concealing stuff that must be stored in the garage provides emotional as well as physical advantages.

3. If you wish to mount or hang frequently-used hand tools (or display them for friends), the smart, practical and economical way is to hang a four-by-eight-foot piece of quarter-inch peg-board on the wall (just like you see in shop displays) – you can do

it easily and a variety of peg hardware is available.

4. Make sure you can see. Most garages are inadequately lit, which makes them feel like a mine shaft instead of part of a home. The wiring is usually adequate; just convert the bare bulb into fluorescent tube lighting. It will make the garage look better and will be safer and cheaper.

5. Paint the garage walls – ninety per cent of garages are unfinished, and thus look naked and shabby. Two coats of a good gloss (new or left over from another job) can be applied for pennies and reward you for years. If the walls are bare, finish with pebble dash.

6. Prepare and seal the floor, if it's concrete. This will make it fast and easy to maintain and improve the looks and feel of the garage.

To seal your garage floor, remove all furniture, tools, etc., from the floor; sweep up all the surface dirt. Mop on a

solution of strong alkaline cleaner, or better still, etching acid diluted in water. (Your janitorial supply house or paint shop has these – with specific directions on the label.) Let it soak in awhile; if the floor is old and marked, you can scrub it with a floor machine. Flush the solution off – preferably using a floor squeegee (see page 136) – and rinse with a hose. Allow the floor to dry for at least five hours, then apply transparent concrete seal or an all-purpose seal, either of which can be obtained at a paint or janitorial supplier. Apply the seal – according to directions – with any applicator that will distribute it in a nice thin even coat, and let it dry. I'd advise a second coat to ensure that all the rough surfaces are filled.

There's no reason to have a garage that embarrasses you. With a little planning and work, it can look like the part of your *home* that it is.

# Do I need a wet/dry vacuum?

Do you *need* a dishwasher? The same is true of a wet/dry vacuum – if you have it, you'll use it to save your time and deterioration in the home. A wet/dry is exactly what its name implies: a vacuum that is capable of sucking up both wet and dry material. Wet/dry vacuums are an everyday commercial tool just beginning to interest the homemaker. They are practical to own and easy to use in the home, and range in cost from £160 (at an electrical appliances shop) to £900 (for a posh commercial one). I'd recommend nothing larger than a five-gallon recovery capacity with a stainless or poly plastic tank. (Non-stainless metal tanks are OK but you have to keep them cleaner so they won't rust between uses.)

A wet/dry vacuum sucks up water (or other liquid) until the tank is full, at which point a float (which is like a rubber ball) will shut off the air pull (suction) and you'll know it's time to empty the tank, in the toilet or garden. For dry jobs, which require using a simple cloth filter, this unit is generally much more efficient and flexible than little household upright or cylinder vacuums, because the hose is larger, the suction flow is stronger, and the attachments are commercial quality.

You probably already know all the dry jobs you can use a vacuum for, but how about some of these *wet* jobs?

1. Picking up floor-scrubbing water (especially out of those cracks and crevices in your floor).
2. Shampooing your own upholstery.
3. Cleaning up food and drink spills before they dry and stain.
4. Picking up vomit, potty, pet mess. (Don't gasp – this is a common and very real cleaning problem.) Cleaning this with a wet/dry is a quick sanitary method. You can then rinse the surface and vacuum the water away. A wet/dry will leave it fresh and clean and odour-free.
5. Picking up sink, bath, and rain floods and overflows inside and outside the house.
6. Emptying (from the top) blocked drains, sinks, toilets, goldfish bowls ...

The most important wet/dry attachments to own are (1) a brush hand tool, (2) an upholstery tool, (3) a rubber-tipped squeegee floor tool. If you have some high areas where dust tends to collect – rough beams or whatever – you can use an extra extension hose. The directions that come with the machine will educate you in minutes as to the basic maintenance needs of the unit.

A £115 professional upright and a £110 commercial wet/dry with attachments is a great home vacuum combination that will last for years if taken care of properly. That's £225 for vacuums that will last you practically forever, and less than you pay for one 'miracle superduper' vacuum.

# As a babysitter, am I obliged to help with cleaning if the house is filthy?

Some time, somewhere all of us are babysitters. People ask you to 'sit' babies and I would advise you to do that first and best and very carefully. If and when the little monsters are snoozing and you have an hour or two before the parents return I would advise you to tackle any mess, whether it's yours or not. There are no rewards in sitting around munching junk food, and watching TV, to kill time, but there are in voluntarily cleaning up. Any 'free' or extra work you do for any-one never goes unnoticed and you won't go unrewarded. You'll build character from service, people will love and respect you and 'tis said in the scriptures, 'He (or she) that has to be commanded in all things is a slothful servant'. My four daughters, during their babysitting years, always cleaned and were always the first four on the list of most wanted sitters in our area. They (like you) gained respect and learnt much, and years later they receive benefits from their efforts. Many young parents need help with more than their children. Don't be afraid to give them some.

123

# I have textured wallpaper and I just can't clean it!

You remove dirt and film from any indented or textured surface in two stages:
  (1) dissolve
  (2) wipe/remove

Too many of us are used to wiping off easy smooth gloss surfaces and forget that *dissolving and suspending* is the number one approach to any cleaning job. Wiping is merely a way of gliding over little pockets full of dirt. If you use the right cleaning solution, the deposit in the grooves will soften and float loose so that a thick terry cloth or a mild brushing action will extract it. Apply a solution of sudsy detergent in warm water to the wallpaper; a lather can be worked up on the vinyl using a soft-bristled brush.

Wait a little, then rinse thoroughly with clean water, changing the water frequently. Give extra attention to removing suds or soap and loosened dirt from the depressed areas of deeply embossed wallpaper. Drying the surface well with a terry towel should absorb any cleaning residue.

Remember, vinyl wallpaper generally contains a chemical compound called a plasticizer. The plasticizer is necessary to condition and soften the vinyl so it can be rolled and hung easily. If dirt is allowed to stay on the surface for a long time, the plasticizer tends to absorb dirt, making the wallpaper even more difficult to clean.

Many stubborn surface stains can be removed with isopropyl alcohol (obtainable from Boots) on a hanky-sized cloth. Do not use lacquer solvents for cleaning vinyl wallpaper.

# Why do people hate housework?

Firstly, because it receives little (if any) appreciation. Secondly, most evidence of cleaning accomplishment literally goes down the drain. Finally, it requires giving a major part of one's lifetime.

It has been accepted and expected that housework has always been present and always has to be done. And 'any old somebody' gets the honour of doing it. We all accept some 'chores' to restore and maintain our lives, but doing the same regular chores without appreciation is discouraging.

Where there is no glory, little personal progress, it is only natural to dislike or even hate it. It's not so much the 'housework' (the physical work) that people hate, it is the amount of personal life time spent doing it that embitters people. Constantly working hard, all day and just being back where you started is not a worthy pursuit and should be changed. I'm a real believer in that. This *can* be changed by reducing the need to clean, *designing* work out, preventing litter, dirt, junk from entering the house, getting equipment that will cut corners, and above all getting those who 'dirty up' to 'clean up' behind themselves.

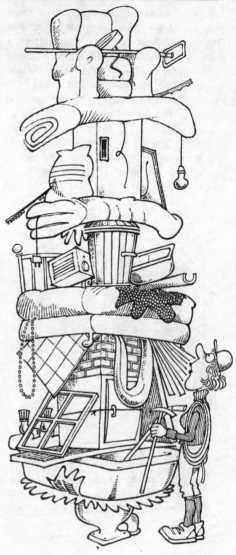

125

# What about those plastic covers for furniture and carpets?

I assume you are referring to the clear plastic runners used over carpeting and the plastic dust covers for upholstered furniture. I think they are the epitome of tattiness as well as a dead loss when it comes to maintenance and cleaning efficiency. If existing surfaces can't be used for what they were intended, why have them? Clear plastic carpet runners are visually offensive and present two different surfaces to be kept clean instead of one. Furniture arm covers (if used) are never on straight – if they're still on the

arm at all. Dust covers, too, often slip or look wrinkled and are never of the same high quality as the furniture they cover. Why pay the price for a nice chair and cover it with a cheap-looking cover?

Plastic covers collect and *show* dust. Why deprive yourself of the pleasure of sinking down into a soft upholstered cushion – who wants to crackle down onto a piece of cold plastic or closely woven canvas cover? You bought the chair to enjoy, not exhibit. Think about that when you're planning your next purchase, and buy what you can comfortably make use of without having to cover. I highly recommend Scotchgard (a soil retardant) for upholstered furniture.

While on the subject, let me also mention self-adhesive shelf paper for cupboards. This 'oilcloth' paper is trickier than you think to apply neatly – and it never stays on neatly very long. When removed, it leaves resins and glue that make for shoddy painting and later, sloppy cupboard shelves. Use good gloss paint or clear varnish to line your shelves – and keep them clean. You'll find that this looks better – and in my opinion it's much more hygienic.

# As an American what is your opinion of British housekeeping?

I toured Britain, visiting buildings and homes when I promoted my first book *Is There Life After Housework?* in 1982. I felt good in British homes: one English woman said, 'We are a wee bit scruffy,' – and that's the way our family lives in America. Our house is there to be used and enjoyed. I liked it. Most British buildings/homes are older, and because of the architecture, are more difficult to clean. The only thing I didn't fall in love with were the tons of knickknacks, dishes, decorations, antiques and mantelpieces, dresser tops and window sills covered with bits and bobs. What a nightmare to clean and protect! I like memories and warmth in a house, but when the home looks like an antique shop, I'm a little uncomfortable and would suggest a good throw-out to your local Oxfam shop. Another improvement that I would suggest to most British people is to keep buildings and homes in a slightly better state of repair. I saw a lot of homes looking unnecessarily rundown because of lack of patching and painting. Mending, redecoration and tasteful replacement makes for less work than repeated *daily* extra cleaning.

# As a professional cleaner, how much would I be worth?

It all depends on how much work you can do in a given amount of time, in a professional manner. Certain jobs have a certain value, but your personal efficiency and technical skill are also important – ultimately, how valuable you are will depend on how fast and how well you can do the job. Most people could make £5-£10 per hour once they have gained true 'professional status' in the housecleaning field. True pro status comes through:

**1. Experience:** Having faced and handled many different types of cleaning challenges – as well as the many types of *people* you have to deal with as a cleaner. Your confidence and competence will develop with experience.

**2. Study:** Finding and reading written material, attending training sessions and lectures, keeping up with new products and methods will all help you to be an efficient cleaner.

**3. Long hours of hard work:** A cleaning business is not a nine to five job. You clean during 'off' hours and lots of them. When competition keeps prices low, more hours of time have to be spent.

Don't work for an hourly wage; everyone is in the habit of thinking a cleaner ought to get a minimum wage and if you ask for an hourly rate higher than that, most customers' faces turn white. Instead, submit a quotation for the work the customer has in mind (see the table on page 124 of *Is There Life After Housework?*) Tell the customer, 'I'll clean all your curtains and blinds and inside windows for £39.50. They like that because they know the cost, with no surprises; you can then work hard, fast, and efficiently, and do it in five hours and make £7.90 per hour. You'll have to charge enough to cover more than your time. Remember: you have the expenses of a phone, vehicle, petrol, supplies, and equipment that will wear out. Occasionally you'll break or ruin something or even underquote for a job or two.

Professional cleaning is a good direction to go. Here are two addresses of professional associations and other technical authorities where you may enquire about cleaning career opportunities, professional training, sources of professional supplies, technique and material updates, etc. They ought to be able to supply almost any cleaning information you want.

1. British Institute of Cleaning Science
   73-74 Central Buildings
   24 Southwark Street
   London SE1 1TY
   Tel: 01-407 2304

2. The Janitorial Suppliers Association
   1 The Glebe
   Worcester Park
   Surrey KT4 7PG
   Tel: 01-330 5970

# But professional cleaning equipment is hard to find...

The amount of time you'll save, plus the quality and safety of professional supplies make it worth the effort to seek them out; they're cheaper in the long run, too, although they may *seem* more expensive because they're often in concentrated form. Most people live within range of a reputable source of cleaning equipment and supplies – they're called janitorial suppliers. Look in the Yellow Pages under 'Janitorial Supplies', or get in touch with the Janitorial Suppliers Association (JANSA, 1 The Glebe, Worcester Park, Surrey KT4 7PG. Tel. 01-330 5970) who keep a list of members and can give you the name of your nearest supplier.

But before you pack the kids, neighbour and Great Aunt Mavis into the car, be sure to ring the supplier about your visit. Check that they sell what you're after – some janitorial supply houses specialise in one or other line of goods, such as catering equipment or cleaning chemicals and don't stock a general selection of housecleaning goods. And you might find that certain items like wet-dry vacs are only available on request. Remember, too, that janitorial suppliers are used to dealing with the trade, but once they know you mean business, they're usually ready and willing to sell directly to you.

When you go into these stores, feel welcome and don't act like a cow in a circus. Act like the professional you are. (You've scrubbed more sinks than a lot of professional cleaners anyway.) The staff will help you choose the best tools for the job at hand and give you expert instruction on how to use them, as well as professional chemicals in the amount you will need. What they don't stock, they can get for you. Most of them buy direct from a factory outlet at a large discount, and on a cash deal most of them will turn around and give you a discount, especially if you gang together with a few of your neighbours for buying power. If you live in a small town like me (where the population is only 620), save up until you get to the big town, then splurge (you should only have to visit the store once a year anyway). And if you just don't feel like visiting a janitorial supplier or your local supplier is inadequate, you can order most items by mail order from Diswinco, 1 Southsea Road, Kingston-on-Thames, Surrey KT1 2EJ (Tel. 01-546 1140/1191). They have made a point of stocking items I've recommended and will know what you're looking for if you mention my books.

Watch the papers under *Miscellaneous — For Sale*, or watch for bankruptcy or business closedowns – used professional cleaning equipment is hard to get rid of, so you'll get some good bargains. I saw a friend pick up a (dirty but in perfect shape) thirteen-inch polisher (£150) for £3. I picked up a £300 floor machine for only £55. Look for a good upright or wet/dry vacuum (preferably the five-gallon size), even mop buckets. The Equipment Chart at the back of the book lists the professional supplies and equipment most likely to be useful to a homeowner. Buy your chemical cleaners in concentrated form and dilute them yourself. The quality of professional materials will save you tons of money and time.

# Are carpet sweepers any good?

A carpet sweeper is a non-electric hand-powered piece of equipment that looks like an anaemic upright vacuum. With a pass or two over the surface, it can whisk bits and pieces from the carpet or floor. You're going to hate me for this next sentence . . . but carpet sweepers are like girdles: they can make the surface look quite impressive, but don't help a bit with the real problem. Because sweepers are fast and produce instant 'clean' results, sweeper lovers have a tendency to use them regularly – and neglect their good beater vacuum, which removes the dirt, sand, pencil lead, crumbs and the like from the depths of the pile. The result is that the rug deteriorates rapidly as the unseen debris below the surface gets to work. If carpet sweepers are only used occasionally or for emergencies (like scooping up scattered crisps between TV programmes or cleaning corn-flakes off the carpet before company arrives), they're great and I could endorse them, but being a realist, I won't have one around my house – to prevent any temptation to give the carpet too many 'once over lightlys!' (And I don't think such infrequent use justifies having the extra appliance. Sorry to have to split up that love affair.

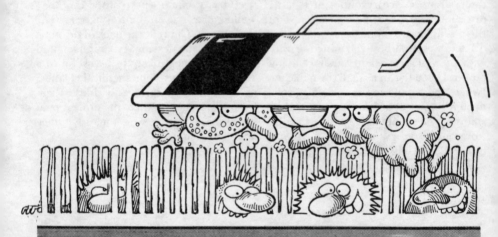

# Is it all worth it?

It most certainly is. That's why you haven't given up before now. Have you noticed that as you improve the quality of your housework, other areas of your life seem to improve? It's called carry-over. Cleaning and organizing a house is one of life's best lessons in self-improvement. You absorb more lessons than a sponge, you're uplifted even as you lift the grime from the garage floor.

The cleanliness level in your house projects your growing pride in youself. The discipline and care with which you remove the dust and cobwebs from the corners of your rooms will carry over into a desire to wipe the cobwebs from the corners of your personality. One of housework's greatest values is its ability to build you into an efficient, appealing person.

A clean house can and will get into a mess again, but you can't make a mess of the improvements in quality of life your efforts have produced. How you live in and care for your home shapes your personality – and your destiny. Home is the centre of civilization. So it's got to be worth it. *It is worth it!*

# Equipment and supplies chart

There *is* life after housework – provided you use the right cleaning equipment and cleaning agents. Forget about supermarkets and stores which stock badly designed and ineffective tools. Professional cleaners zip through several three-storey buildings in a day – because they use professional equipment.

Throughout the country there are janitorial supply houses which provide contract cleaners with all their needs. On page 130 under the heading 'But professional equipment is hard to find' I have covered this problem fully. Remember that if you can't find local suppliers you can obtain most of the items by mail order from Diswinco Supplies Ltd, 1 Southsea Road, Kingston-on-Thames, Surrey KT1 2EJ (Tel. 01-546 1140/1191). They supply all the products on this chart except those marked *.

The basic janitorial cleaning compounds described in this chart and throughout the book do not all have child-proof lids – so make sure you keep them out of the reach of small children.

| ITEM | SIZE | TYPE | USE | SOURCE |
|---|---|---|---|---|
| **Kentucky mop** | 16 oz. | yarn with clip-on handle | Used for all hard-surface floors (concrete too). Heads can be changed in seconds. | janitorial supply house |
| **Dustmop** | 18" | cotton with rotating (or movable) handle | All hard floors. Fast and efficient; lasts for years. Treat occasionally with dust mop oil – 1 bottle will last 6 years. Launder and re-treat when saturated with dirt. | janitorial supply house |
| **Mop bucket** | 2½/3 gallons | metal or plastic with self-contained roller wringer | With self-contained roller for wringing (saves hand injuries) used for mopping, wall washing, mixing, and a punch bowl at a cleaner's wedding. Wheels can be dangerous. | janitorial supply house |
| ***Cleaning cloth** | 9" x 18" | white towel cloth (cotton) | Replaces the rag – used for all cleaning jobs; especially effective in wall and ceiling cleaning. Fold and turn inside out for 16 cleaning surfaces. Made at home from towelling. | white towelling from some good department stores |

134

| ITEM | SIZE | TYPE | USE | SOURCE |
|------|------|------|-----|--------|
| **Dry sponge** | 5"x7"x½" | chemically treated rubber | Use on flat wall and ceiling surfaces and wallpaper – fold in hand under knuckles for even use. Discard when black or soiled. Keep it packaged when stored. Never get it wet. | only from Diswinco |
| **Toilet brush** | 4"x6" | black nylon | To scrub inside the toilet bowl to keep it free of hard water mineral deposit build up. | janitorial supply house |
| **Spray bottle** | 2 pints | plastic, trigger spray | To fill with diluted concentrates for hand-spray work on spots, bathroom, windows and any small cleaning duty. Several of these around the house would be a good investment. Smaller sizes are less efficient but easily available. | janitorial supply house |
| **Squeegee** | 12" or 14" | brass or stainless steel Ettore | Strictly for window cleaning. Avoid contact with rough surfaces to keep rubber blade perfectly sharp. A telescopic pole, for extending the handle, is obtainable. | janitorial supply house |
| **\*Bowl swab** | 3" ball cotton | wooden handle | Used to force water out of toilet bowl and to swab the bowl with cleaner. (See pages 116/117.) Difficult to find. Some toilets can be emptied by plunging with a brush. Can be home-made. | janitorial supply house |
| **\*Elbie Dustless Duster** | 20"x20" | treated cloth | Used for dusting. The cloth is specially treated so that it collects dust without scattering. There is no need to shake out the cloth and it does not leave an oil residue. Supplies from Batley & Co. Tel: 061-480 3880. | some hardware stores and department stores |

| ITEM | SIZE | TYPE | USE | SOURCE |
|---|---|---|---|---|
| *Scrubbing sponge | 3″x4″x1″ 3″x6″x1″ | pink/white or blue/white nylon | Use where limited abrasion is needed. Always wet before using. Squeeze – don't wring. Use Scotchbrite's pink sponge for delicate surfaces. Their blue sponge is good in bathrooms. | hardware or department store |
| Wet-dry vacuum | 5 gallons | metal or plastic tank | Use this for all hand-work vacuuming; to vacuum up water when scrubbing floor; for over-flows, spills. (Get squeegee, upholstery and edge-tool attach-ments with it.) You may choose a smaller model which is available in many electrical shops. | commercial models from janitorial supply house |
| Upright vacuum | 12″ 6 amps | commercial model with cloth bag | Basically for carpet-rug vacuuming. Don't buy half a dozen attachments; get a long cord. | janitorial supply house |
| Doodlebug | 5″x10″ pad | hand tool with pad | To clean edges of hard-surface floors. Wash out and dry after use. Different pads for tough, medium or light jobs. | janitorial supply house |
| Floor squeegee | 18″ | push-pull brass/stain-less steel | For floor cleaning, removing water and drying paths or garage floors. Ettore brand. Replacement rubber blades available. | janitorial supply house |
| Mats | 3′x4′, 3′x5′, or 4′x6′. Rolls 3′ and 4′ wide | Polypropylane fibre pile, polyester primary backing on vinyl base | Use Jaymart's 'Tuf-n-Tidy II' or 'Caretaker' as entrance matting. Help to remove dust and particles from shoes and clothing, absorb mud and water from foot traffic. Available in different lengths 3′, 4′ or 6′ wide – in various colours. Samples available from Jaymart, Tel: Westbury (0373) 864926. | order from janitorial supply house or carpet shops |

| ITEM | SIZE | TYPE | USE | SOURCE |
|---|---|---|---|---|
| **Concrete seal** | 5 litres | resin based or inorganic-chemical based | Used to seal floor so that concrete dust is not continually trodden into other areas of the house. Concrete paint/seal is available in many colours. | janitorial supply house, builders' merchants |
| **Etching acid** | 5 litres | concentrate | For cleaning and etching a concrete floor before sealing. For removing both surface lime and dirt. Note: A strong concentrated alkaline cleaner can be used instead. | janitorial supply house, builders' merchants |
| **Disinfectant cleaner** | 5 litres | concentrate/quaternary | Dilute with water for use in bathroom cleaning or mopping wherever sanitation is essential. It is a neutral cleaner and can be used for general household jobs. | janitorial supply house |
| **Neutral cleaner** | 5 litres | concentrate without disinfectant | For mopping, damp-mopping, spray cleaning paintwork, cleaning panelling and all general cleaning where a disinfectant is not needed. | janitorial supply house |
| **Wax remover/ stripper** | 5 litres | ammoniated | To remove wax from a floor. Apply generously with mop onto the floor. You will need to use a Doodlebug or floor machine to dislodge the old wax. | janitorial supply house |
| **Furniture polish** | standard aerosol can | water or oil wax emulsion aerosol | Use spray polish only where finish does not maintain its own lustre. Sparkle or Mr. Sheen are aerosols of this special kind. | supermarkets, hardware stores |
| **Emulsion floor polish** | 1 gallon or 5 litres | metallised dry-bright liquid | Hard floor surfaces, tiles, linoleum and sealed concrete. | janitorial supply house |

# Index

# Why do you carry a loo suitcase?

Doctors carry little black bags; lawyers and business executives carry attaché cases; I carry a toilet suitcase because I'm a professional cleaner. The toilet, which I clean regularly (as do a million other professional cleaners and fifteen million homemakers), is a symbol of my trade. I carry it to dispel any doubt as to how I feel about my profession – I'm proud of it.

(I'll admit, however, that when I meet a business contact and reach in my suitcase to get a business card, nobody will take it! And there's always a lot of suspense when it bumps out of the carousel chute at airports as people wait to see who will claim it.)

Twenty-five years ago I started my cleaning career to pay for my university education. I put an ad in the local paper and homeowners began to call me. I shrank a few carpets and streaked some walls and floors at first, but the women whose homes I cleaned taught me as I went along. As I learned, I worked faster and developed new techniques for streamlining cleaning tasks – while still getting the job done well. I hired fellow students and named my growing company Varsity Contractors. Wanting to expand my business beyond homes, I landed a contract to clean the Bell Telephone building in our town – a big account. Today, Varsity Contractors is a multi-million dollar business with offices in thirteen states.

Not forgetting where I got my start, it was only natural that I try to repay the wonderful homemakers who taught me the basics of cleaning. So I began giving seminars to women's groups across the country, showing them how to use professional cleaning products and techniques to save up to seventy five per cent of the time they spent on housework. I also wanted to help homemakers be as proud of their profession as they should be.

I've been nicknamed by the media: 'The Billy Graham of the Pine-Sol Set,' 'King of the Toilet Ring,' 'The Urinal Colonel,' 'Fastest Bowl Brush in the West,' and 'The Pied Piper of Purification.' But I have the last laugh as I watch other businessmen trying to balance attaché cases, coats, and umbrellas while trying to read their morning paper. I just sit on my toilet suitcase and read my *Wall Street Journal!*

Don A. Aslett

141